D1774462

LC   GREENE
1011   The meaning of the 62061
G73   humanities
1969

DE ANZA COLLEGE LEARNING CENTER
21250 Stevens Creek Blvd.
Cupertino, CA 95014

PRINTED IN U.S.A.   23-362-002

THE MEANING
OF THE
HUMANITIES

THE MEANING OF THE HUMANITIES

FIVE ESSAYS BY

RALPH BARTON PERRY
AUGUST CHARLES KREY
ERWIN PANOFSKY
ROBERT LOWRY CALHOUN
GILBERT CHINARD

WITH A PREFACE BY
ROBERT KILBURN ROOT

EDITED WITH AN INTRODUCTION BY
THEODORE MEYER GREENE

KENNIKAT PRESS/PORT WASHINGTON, N. Y.

THE MEANING OF THE HUMANITIES

Copyright 1938 by Princeton University Press
Reissued in 1969 by Kennikat Press by arrangement with Princeton University Press
Library of Congress Catalog Card No: 73-86020
SBN 8046-0562-9

Manufactured by Taylor Publishing Company   Dallas, Texas
ESSAY AND GENERAL LITERATURE INDEX REPRINT SERIES

PREFACE

THE great humanists of the later Middle Ages and the Renaissance would have been puzzled by our modern partition of the liberal arts into so-called divisions of mathematics and science, social studies, and the humanities. Though each of the seven arts which made up the *quadrivium* and *trivium* in their schools and universities had its own appropriate subject matter, all seven, geometry and astronomy no less than rhetoric and dialectic, had one single function—that of developing and training human intelligence so that, freed from the mists of ignorance and prejudice, man might live a life of more abundant goodness. The humanist of today can no longer be a universal doctor; knowledge is now so multifarious that no one can make the whole of it his province. But the present-day humanist is still concerned to see that learning does not wholly forget its unifying purpose, that facts shall take on significance, that the various elements which make up the life of the individual and of society as a whole shall be justly appraised, and that knowledge may thus flower and fructify into true wisdom. To further this discipline of humane interpretation is still one of the primary duties of a university, and a duty which those responsible for university policy must never forget.

It was with these ideas in mind that the Princeton University Committee on Public Lectures determined that for the academic year 1937-1938 the Spencer Trask Lectures should be devoted to a consideration of the Meaning of the Humanities. Five distinguished scholars were invited to contribute, each from the field of his own more special studies, to a symposium of humanistic interpretation. These lectures, which were delivered in the late winter and early spring of 1938, have now been brought together in this book. The Princeton University Press earnestly hopes that it may be able to publish in subsequent years other volumes of humanistic studies similarly conceived.

The five scholars invited to participate in this symposium are of widely diverse interests and training. Ralph Barton Perry is a graduate of Princeton who did his advanced study at Harvard, where he is now Professor of Philosophy. August Charles Krey was trained in the University of Wisconsin, and has been since 1913 Professor of History in the University of Minnesota. Erwin Panofsky received his doctoral degree from the University of Freiburg (Breisgau), served as Professor of Art in the University of Hamburg from 1921 to 1933, has been Visiting Professor in New York University and Visiting Lecturer in Princeton University, and is now a member of the staff of the Princeton Institute for Advanced Study. Robert Lowry Calhoun received his undergraduate training at Carlton College, and his graduate training chiefly at Yale. After two years of teaching at Carlton, he has been since 1923 a member of the Yale Faculty. Gilbert Chinard was trained in the University of Bordeaux and at the Sorbonne. Since 1908 he has taught at a number of American universities—the College of the City of New York, Brown University, the University of California, and Johns Hopkins. Since 1937 he has been Meredith Howland Pyne Professor of French Literature at Princeton. He is a member of the Legion of Honor and is Lauréat of the French Academy.

It is highly appropriate that a book on the Meaning of the Humanities should be the fruit of such a wide diversity of gifts; for diversity is in itself one of the characters of the humanistic spirit, which seeks for universality, but never for uniformity. As the reader turns from one lecture to the next he will find, as he will expect to find, divergencies of opinion; but he will also find throughout a single unity of underlying purpose. The five lectures as here printed have been arranged in an order of sequence, somewhat different from the order of their oral delivery, which serves to point up their essential unity.

When the course of lectures had been completed, their substance was discussed in an open forum presided over by Theodore M. Greene, Professor of Philosophy at Princeton, who had already taken chief part in planning the series and in keeping the various lecturers informed of one another's ideas. By his good offices of mediation, what might have been merely a series became a true symposium. It is, therefore, very fitting that he should be the editor of this volume. To it he has contributed also an introductory essay which analyzes the general concept of humanistic culture in such fashion as to relate the five lectures in a single harmonious perspective, and to enhance greatly their essential unity.

To the five lecturers and their editor and introducer, whose cooperation has made this book possible, Princeton University is deeply grateful.

ROBERT KILBURN ROOT
Dean of the Faculty of Princeton University

CONTENTS

	PAGE
Preface	v
Introduction	xi
A Definition of the Humanities *By* Ralph Barton Perry	1
History and the Humanities *By* August Charles Krey	43
The History of Art as a Humanistic Discipline *By* Erwin Panofsky	89
Theology and the Humanities *By* Robert Lowry Calhoun	119
Literature and the Humanities *By* Gilbert Chinard	151
Index of Proper Names and Titles	171

INTRODUCTION
By THEODORE MEYER GREENE

INTRODUCTION

THE title of this volume, "The Meaning of the Humanities," is happily ambiguous, for the term "meaning" has a dual connotation. It raises, on the one hand, the question of what the word "humanities" refers to, and, on the other, the question of the significance or value of that to which the word refers. The title constitutes, in short, an invitation to consider both the *nature* of the humanities and their *worth* for man.

The reader will discover that all of the ensuing essays discuss, with varying emphases, both the nature and the significance of the humanities. But the authors, distinguished scholars each in his own field, have approached these problems in terms of their respective disciplines; each essay reflects not only the writer's temperament but his professional interest. They differ, accordingly, in specific orientation, and the primary emphasis is systematic in some cases, historical in others. These complementary approaches and the somewhat different underlying *Weltanschauungen* contribute notably to the interest of the book as a whole. It is, indeed, peculiarly appropriate that a volume on the meaning of the humanities should itself so eloquently exemplify one of the essential characteristics of the humanistic outlook, namely, the recognition of and respect for human diversity. For in the very act of disagreeing with one another, humanists, *qua* humanists, must insist on the right and duty of every responsible thinker to pursue his inquiries in his own way and to assess human life and its complex environment without social threat or coercion. That humanism is fundamentally individualistic in this sense is accepted here as a basic postulate and is defended in various ways in the subsequent essays.

Any attempt, therefore, to minimize the divergencies which characterize these essays would be not only presumptuous but contrary to the spirit of the humanistic enterprise. The only unity which we as humanists can prize is a unity *amid* diversity, a unity which reflects the rich variety and novelty of human life itself. Mere difference and novelty, however, are as little valued by the true humanist as are mere arbitrary uniformity and empty oneness. As finite human beings, each with his own temperamental, professional and cultural perspective, men are bound to differ, and the humanist, above all others, attaches importance to these differences of perspective and belief; yet this very attitude of respect for human individuality implies a basic agreement concerning human personality itself and the conditions of its growth. This agreement, however, is often more implicit than explicit, and the individualism so basic to humanistic endeavor acts as a powerful centrifugal force, making too often for unnecessary and tragic discord. Hence the need for a clearer definition of the humanists' common objective and a more adequate understanding of the means whereby this objective may be realized.

The need for such a re-examination of basic issues is perennial, but it is peculiarly pressing today. For the whole world is drifting or being driven with ever greater acceleration into a state profoundly antagonistic to the values which the humanist most sincerely cherishes. Social mechanization, whether industrial, political or militaristic, threatens increasingly that freedom of thought and responsible action which is the very condition of human dignity. This world-wide trend is in part the result of economic and other causes which continue to baffle our understanding; both individually and collectively we are in many ways the helpless victims of forces which still defy successful control. In part, however, the contemporary threat to human values lies in the deliberate activities of certain individuals and groups whose ideologies are monopolistic and totalitarian and who, in one way or another, have acquired autocratic power in our society. These men are so powerful, in turn, because they are motivated by well defined immediate objectives and because they have succeeded in arousing in their supporters a passionate and uncritical devotion to a "common" cause. The modern scene testifies with tragic eloquence to the immediate effectiveness of this anti-humanistic strategy.

In his attempt to combat this threat to human integrity and worth, the modern humanist, like his predecessors in other ages and cultures, is at a grave disadvantage. If he fights fire with fire, his own weapons, borrowed from his opponent, will presently destroy him, and any immediate victory that he may gain will be indistinguishable from defeat. His objective is extraordinarily difficult of attainment. For he is by definition an individualist; and the uncoordinated activities of individuals are notoriously ineffective in a regimented society. He is a natural aristocrat in taste and in sensitiveness to the finer values; and in every society, truly imaginative individuals unhappily constitute a minority. He is committed to reflective scrutiny and criticism; yet the pressure of immediate circumstance seems to demand quick decision and unswerving, uncritical allegiance to an aggressive social program. The life of humanistic wisdom and enjoyment demands, in short, both security and leisure, and where, today, are security and leisure to be found in combination? Ours is a society of immediate objectives and therefore a society in which loyalty to basic ideals, the creation and appreciation of artistic and literary values, and the patient search for an historical and philosophical perspective appear not as the fundamental human necessities which they are, but as luxuries that man can ill afford. Hence to the modern "realist" the humanist seems to be an irresponsible child playing on the brink of an active volcano.

Humanism can defend itself against this charge of irresponsibility and futility by challenging the ultimate realism of the self-styled "realist." Even the dictator professes allegiance, whether sincerely or hypocritically, to the ideal of human welfare. The crucial issue resolves itself therefore into the question: What are the nature and conditions of man's true well-being? That such well-being is in part a function of physical health and economic security will not be questioned by either party. What is in question is the whole set of moral, aesthetic and religious values which modern dictators misinterpret and twist to their own ends, but which the humanist regards as the very cornerstone of liberty and culture. The humanist's answer to the modern "realist," in short, is to accuse *him* of building his house on sand, with his worship of false gods, his defense of spurious art, and, above all, his denial of that spiritual freedom which is man's most precious moral and intellectual heritage.

If we are not to be overwhelmed today by mob hysteria and anti-humanistic propaganda, humanists must, as Thomas Mann has urged, become "militant" and boldly proclaim the faith that is in them. They cannot, however, hope for immediate or spectacular success; they cannot avert a sudden social cataclysm, if that is the fate presently in store for us. It is also of the utmost importance that we preserve our historical and philosophical perspective and conceive of man's age-old humanistic endeavor as an end in itself and not merely as a means of resisting modern authoritarian tyranny. We must remember that the humanistic ideal is as enduring as human life itself and that steadfast loyalty to this ideal is integral to human dignity in all ages and all cultures alike. Now, as ever, our chief concern must be not the changing scene or the passing crisis but rather the nature of the human spirit in its eternal quest for enduring values. We must seek to preserve what the human race has culturally achieved and we must build slowly and laboriously for a more distant

Introduction   xvii

future. The humanistic edifice will be secure, meanwhile, only in proportion as it rests on the firm foundation of well defined principles and clearly envisaged ends. To discover these principles and ends, in the spirit not of blinding indoctrination but of a liberal education, is the humanist's traditional and immediate responsibility.

This responsibility can ultimately be met only through the efforts of thoughtful and devoted individuals. But humanists can be of invaluable assistance to one another. Indeed, theirs is a task which demands cooperation among "experts" in the several humanistic disciplines—not goose-step uniformity, but willing cooperation of free and responsible agents who, while respecting divergence of opinion, are yet resolved to articulate and clarify their common allegiance to a common objective. The present volume represents a contribution to this venture. Its authors have made no attempt to draft a definitive humanistic program. Their endeavor has been rather to explore basic issues and ask crucial questions. They were unable to consult with one another before submitting their manuscripts to the press; hence such agreement as emerges is spontaneous, not calculated. Only the editor has had the advantage of reading all the essays prior to publication. It is therefore his privilege to attempt a more synoptic synthesis, and for this attempt he alone is responsible. It is his hope that the following brief analysis of the concept of human culture and of the application of this concept to the notion of a liberal education may in some measure relate the subsequent essays in a single perspective.

The thesis I should like to propose is that education is liberal in proportion as it promotes genuine culture, that culture is a function of the success with which available empirical data, in all their variety and multiplicity, are both historically oriented and philosophically interpreted, and that culture, so defined, is the ultimate goal of all humanistic endeavor.

It is clear that the term "culture" is here used in a normative sense to signify a qualitative standard or ideal of human aspiration, not in the purely generic sense in which it is often quite legitimately employed by anthropologists and sociologists.[1] The concept of human culture, in contradistinction to that of diverse "culture patterns" as geographic and temporal social phenomena, is the concept of the ideally good life, that is, of human experience in its highest and most complete potential manifestations.

The many conflicting accounts of the good life which history has recorded testify to the elusiveness of this normative ideal. No exhaustive analysis can here be attempted. I can, however, try to indicate some of the more crucial aspects of human nature and experience with which all humanists must, I believe, come to terms in any comprehensive interpretation of culture and a liberal education.

This analysis will involve distinguishing five "levels" of human experience. The first two levels, which may for convenience be entitled the levels of "atomistic awareness" and "solitary synthesis," are frankly figments of the imagination; they have an expository value but are, so far as we know, never perfectly exemplified in actuality. The third and fourth levels, which I shall call the levels of "social convention" and "creative and critical specialization," are actual and familiar. The fifth level, that of "cultural or historico-philosophical synthesis," is ideal and therefore only partly actualized, since it constitutes the highest objective of all humanistic thought and

---

[1] Anthropologists and sociologists are becoming increasingly aware that every culture, however primitive, has factual and normative aspects *both* of which deserve explicit consideration. Note, for example, the distinction that is sometimes made between "civilization" (as a merely descriptive concept) and "culture" (as a more normative concept).

Introduction   xix

action. The humanist, I shall argue, is uniquely defined in terms of his allegiance to this ideal, whose attainment constitutes, as he believes, man's true ambition as a human being. Those, on the other hand, who repudiate this ideal will be found to define the goal of human endeavor in terms of the third or fourth levels of experience. The humanist recognizes, of course, that a perfect cultural synthesis permits of only partial realization by even the most cultured members of any society and that it can be comprehended only fitfully by the wisest of men in any age. But, for this very reason, it is the peculiar obligation of all sincere humanists to envisage this cultural ideal as clearly as they can and to make every effort to translate it so far as possible into actuality.

1. Starting, then, with the lowest level of conscious awareness, let us conceive of a living organism wholly devoid of memory, reason and imagination, but possessed of man's normal capacity for sensation, emotion and the feelings of pleasure and pain. What would be the "experience" of such a sentient being? The answer is evident. Incapable of memory, it would be wholly unaware of a past even though it continued to exist over a period of time. Lacking all sense of the past, it could have no awareness of the present as present, though each of its sensations, emotions and feelings would, at the moment of occurrence, be described by us as instances of present awareness. And in the absence of both memory and imagination it could have no sense of a future and would therefore be quite incapable of purposive thought or conduct. Furthermore, it would lack the ability to observe and interpret similarities and differences in its external environment or in its own inner states. It could only be aware of specific sense data in their discrete particularity and could have no apprehension of "objects" as individual and enduring patterns. And though capable of momentary emotional response and sensitive to fleeting pleasures and

pains, it could not judge these emotions and feelings either quantitatively or qualitatively, and could therefore have no sense of comparative values.

Such a being, then, would lack all sense of temporal and spatial order and would be completely incapable of chronological perspective and systematic interpretation; it would have no power of discrimination and comparison and could therefore have no intelligible apprehension of its physical environment, no sense of values, and no interests or purposes, ideals or practical objectives. Its "experience" would therefore differ profoundly from our everyday human experience; its "world" would be a mere succession of meaningless particulars (or "brute facts," in the language of philosophical analysis) and its only mode of cognition would be mere "atomistic awareness."

It is of course possible that certain actually existing primitive organisms do possess some such conscious awareness. And man himself, as a normal human being, may approach this sub-human state in moments of extreme exhaustion or at the instant before falling asleep, though even then his consciousness would be infinitely richer and more highly organized than that of the fantastic creature whom we have just depicted. But whether or not such atomistic awareness actually occurs is irrelevant to our argument, whose purpose is merely to exhibit as vividly as possible the essential ingredients contributing to human culture and the ideally good life.

2. Let us consider next the case of a conscious being who is not only capable of sensation, feeling and emotion but is also endowed with the faculties of memory, reason and imagination, but who, from the moment of birth, has been deprived of all contact with human society. This is a variant of the philosophical fiction of the solitary mind, or, in more picturesque terms, of a man with normal innate endowment condemned from earliest infancy to a life of solitude on a

tropical island. What would be the "experience" of such a fictitious individual and how would it differ from mere "atomistic awareness"?

First of all, such a solitary mind could have a sense of time. Possessed of memory, it could recall some of its own past experiences and be aware of itself as living at each instant in the "present"; and, by an act of the imagination, it could envisage a not-yet-present, that is, an immediate and even a somewhat more distant future. Again, with the aid of memory and reason it could discriminate and compare its own successive inner and outer experiences. It could note the recurrent sensory qualities and patterns in its physical environment and perceive individual "objects" or things, apprehend both their uniqueness and their similiarities and differences, and recognize the coercive spatio-temporal order of their appearance. It could also remember some of its own feelings of pleasure and pain in specific contexts and learn to avoid situations productive of pain and to re-occasion situations conducive to pleasure. Its emotional responses would be correspondingly modified and enriched by its own earlier responses and memories. It could thus develop more and more varied and enduring interests and act in an increasingly purposive manner. And, finally, with the establishment of useful habits and through a partial mastery of its physical environment, such a being might eventually achieve some measure of security and leisure. It might therefore, on occasion, indulge in a primitive type of speculation regarding its own nature and destiny. And if we suppose it to be capable of aesthetic and religious response to its environment, it might, on the one hand, employ its leisure to adorn itself and to create simple patterns of color and sound for its own amusement, and on the other hand, occasionally feel that sense of the eerie, the strange and the mysterious which students of religion regard as the psychological raw material of man's developed consciousness of the divine. In a word, such a solitary being would be able, at least theoretically, to have all of man's primitive experiences save those that involve man's relation to his fellow-men, and it could organize these experiences, both chronologically and systematically, as completely as would be possible for a single individual in a single lifetime. Its "world" would no longer be a mere chaos of particulars but the primitive beginning of an orderly cosmos.

And yet, even though we endow this solitary mind with the combined innate capacities of a scientific, artistic, religious and speculative genius, we cannot, by the wildest stretch of the imagination, attribute to it more than the most rudimentary experience as measured by ordinary human standards. For note the inescapable limitations to which such a mind would be subjected, limitations occasioned by its lack of social traditions and institutions. In youth and in maturity it would have to face the world wholly unaided by other human beings. It would inherit no implements for the mastery of its environment and no shelter from the elements. It would receive no assistance in its interpretation of natural events. It would be taught no language and would therefore possess no vehicle for the recording of its observations or the articulation of its rudimentary interpretations. Its awareness of time would thus not only be limited to the span of its own memories; unless it succeeded in inventing some means of recording its own experiences (and what incentive could it have to do so if it had no companions with whom it might communicate?) its past would slip away from it almost unnoticed.

Because of these handicaps, a solitary mind could therefore organize its moment to moment experiences only in a most rudimentary fashion. Its adaptation to its environment would actually be inferior to that of animals, who are equipped with specialized instincts and who, in addition, receive parental and social training. It would be superior to animals only to the extent to which it could, unaided and in a single lifetime, achieve a minute fraction of what the human race has achieved cooperatively through countless ages and has preserved in language, tradition and social institutions. It would, in short, not only be entirely devoid of morality; it would, whatever its native endowment, utterly lack human culture and be doomed to an existence infinitely inferior to that of the most primitive and stupid savage.

3. This imaginary being has been invented to set in relief our incalculable indebtedness to our social heritage. Man, we are told, climbs his own ancestral tree; and just as, biologically, ontogenesis recapitulates philogenesis, so, culturally, man is actually born into a social inheritance which he must rapidly assimilate if he is to rise above sub-human barbarism and become a human being. The level of "experience" which we must next examine is therefore that of "social convention."

To describe this level in detail would involve a survey of all the generic characteristics of man as a social being and of the incredibly complex society of which he is a part. Fortunately it will suffice for our purpose merely to mention those familiar characteristics which serve to distinguish normal human experience from that of an hypothetical solitary mind. These characteristics are embraced in the terms language, tradition and institution.

A language may, in the present context, be defined as any vehicle, adopted by convention, which is suited to the purpose of organizing, recording and communicating human thought and experience. The most flexible type of language is the verbal type, but gestures and other bodily movements are also linguistic vehicles, as are works of art in each of the several artistic media. The interesting distinctions between different types of language are of less importance for us, however, than is the distinction between language as a vehicle for immediate thought and communication and language as employed for a more or less permanent and objective human record. This distinction is exemplified in the relation of the spoken to the written word. The spoken word (and its artistic and other equivalents) suffices for the establishment and preservation of social traditions in a primitive society. With the aid of human records, however, man is not only able to elaborate and express his ideas with far greater power, but to preserve his cultural achievements with more completeness over a longer period of time. Indeed, history (in contrast to mere word-of-mouth tradition) became possible only with the invention of human records. Without such records man can only be dimly aware of his indebtedness to his own past and can only partially come into his cultural inheritance.

Under the category of tradition must be subsumed all that the human race succeeds in preserving, by whatever method, and in making available to successive generations. The sum-total of traditions in any society is thus the whole body of custom and folk-lore, whether moral or utilitarian, aesthetic, religious or speculative, that is available to an individual born into that society. As we have already suggested, one of the essential vehicles for social tradition is language. A second and complementary vehicle is the aggregate of social institutions.

Even animals, as we are well aware, are driven by instinct to various types of social organization such as the shoal, the herd and the family, and in the case of such creatures as ants and bees this organization is highly intricate and marvelously regimented. These instinctive societies are the prototype of human institutions if we consider primarily their conventional and static character. For institutions are essentially conservative; their basic function is to preserve the painfully acquired wisdom which individual vagary would ignore or destroy. Without them, the members of a social group would quickly drift into the predicament of the solitary mind; it is only through such institutions as the family and the state, the school and the church, that the wisdom which the human race has laboriously acquired and cherished can be made available to its members in successive periods.

The conservatism of social institutions, in turn, provides the key to the most striking characteristic of human experience at the level of social convention, namely, its orthodoxy. Such experience is entirely moulded by traditions and conforms in all essential respects to dominant social patterns. Each of us lives at this conventional level most of the time, for we are creatures of social habit. Our religious beliefs and practices, our political creeds, our aesthetic preferences, our moral codes, and even our interpretations of nature are but the echoes of our social environment. Even the most original and gifted of men are in large measure what society has made them.

The incalculable value to man of these cumulative social influences needs no detailed elaboration. They produce what the sociologist calls a "culture pattern," and it is largely through the assimilation of such a pattern that man in any society can acquire whatever culture in the normative sense he succeeds in attaining. We are not only *what* we are because of the cultural heritage into which we have been born; our lives are as *rich* or as *impoverished* as they are largely because of the cultural value, or lack of value, of the particular culture pattern in which we find ourselves.

The wholly conventional individual, meanwhile, is again partly an abstraction. For even the most submissive and unimaginative of mortals has some capacity for original creation and criticism. Similarly, no living society is wholly static; new social problems demand new solutions and old established conventions become inadequate and require modification. These changes, in turn, are possible because the more original members of every society are forever contributing to it new ideas, new instruments and new evaluations. Indeed, the very traditions whose perpetuation constitutes social orthodoxy have usually originated in the earlier discoveries of outstanding individuals. Thus religious traditions and institutions reflect the insights and the interpretative and organizing genius of great religious leaders of a former day, and the layman's interpretations of nature in one generation are but the popularized versions of the discoveries of scientific genius in an earlier time. In short, if society is not to perish from stagnation, its hallowed conventions must undergo continual transformation, and if an individual is to remain spiritually alive he must exercise whatever capacity he has for criticism and initiative.

4. A consideration of the forces that make for vitality and growth in a society and in an individual brings us to the fourth level of "experience," the level of "creative and critical specialization." Pure specialization, like absolute conformity to convention, is again an abstraction, since no individual or society is entirely given to specialization. Like social convention, however, it manifests itself in all human individuals and societies. Though neither type of experience ever appears in complete isolation, each is an essential generic characteristic of the thought and activities of the human race.

Even the most primitive of human societies is based on functional specialization. Plato recognized this centuries ago in his classic account, in the *Republic,* of the origin and structure of a community. Men, he reminds us, have, on the one hand, a variety of needs and, on the other, a diversity of aptitudes. Hence, in an ideal community, each member of the group should be trained to a mastery of that technique and to the performance of that task for which he is temperamentally best fitted, provided that his labors conduce to the common good. No actual society has done more than approximate to this ideal. Every known culture, however, has exemplified in some measure the principle of the division of labor.

Introduction   xxvii

Again, all societies indulge in a variety of corporate activities which reflect mankind's chief generic interests. Thus in primitive societies man's interest in other human beings and his need for cooperating with his fellows manifests itself in such institutions as the family and the clan, in taboo and social ritual, and in innumerable practices relating to property rights and personal safety. His concern with the supernatural expresses itself in legend and religious ritual. His aesthetic impulse shows itself in bodily decoration, ceramic design, song and dance. He even exhibits in myth and poetry a primitive interest in his social past, and, on occasion, a more synoptic curiosity regarding the nature of reality as a whole and the purpose and destiny of human life. No adequate anthropological account of a primitive culture can fail to differentiate between these diverse though closely interrelated human interests as revealed in social mores and institutions.

In our own society the generic interests, thoughts and activities of the common man (and each of us is a common man in most respects) are similarly diversified, however much these distinguishable factors are fused in every concrete situation. This generic diversification is mirrored in such social institutions as the family, state, church, school, press, museum and concert-hall. This is the common soil which nourishes individual specialization. Were man's basic interests not themselves diverse, individual specialization in art and science, religion and politics, history and philosophy, would be psychologically and socially impossible.

Specialization, then, is present in every society, however primitive or advanced. The term "specialization," however, is normally applied only to the more developed types of specialized activity and thought indulged in by certain individuals in more complex and diversified cultures such as ours. The fourth level of experience, which we must now try to analyze, manifests itself most clearly in specialization of this type. It will be found to exhibit characteristics of vital import to the humanist.

A specialist in this narrower sense may be defined as a man who has extensively cultivated a particular aptitude and who, inspired by one of the generic interests of mankind and equipped with an appropriate technique, is able to indulge to an unusual degree in creative or critical activity in his chosen field. The adjectives "creative" and "critical" indicate two aspects of specialization which actually complement one another but either of which can receive primary emphasis. Each, entirely divorced from the other, is unproductive; creation wholly undisciplined by critical analysis and evaluation runs riot and issues in mere ebullient novelty, while criticism which is not vitalized by the creative imagination and which is not concerned with man's creative products feeds on itself and ends in sterility. The greatest achievements of mankind have been brought about by the disciplined imagination, that is, by original invention and constructive criticism functioning as aspects of a single organic process. Thus the world's greatest statesmen, moral and religious leaders, artists and scientists, historians and philosophers, have invariably possessed unusual creative powers unusually disciplined by critical reflection. None the less, specialists have tended to be primarily original thinkers or primarily critics. Thus religion has had its saints and its theologians, politics its statesmen and its political philosophers, art its artists and its critics, and even science its original investigators and its critical theorists. The more extreme this type of specialization, meanwhile, the more urgent the need for effective cooperation between specialists of every type.

It is inevitable that as a society grows more complex, and as its needs, interests and cultural achievements become more numerous and diversified, a tendency to ever-increasing specialization should manifest itself. This is strikingly exemplified in our western culture. Since notable advance in any subject involves a mastery of all relevant facts and techniques, no single individual today, however brilliant and industrious, can possibly hope to excel in more than one of the major fields of human interest. Indeed most of these fields are themselves too intricate to permit of mastery by a single individual in a single lifetime. Hence the growing tendency to specialize still further—for example, not only in mathematics but in some delimited region of mathematics, not only in one of the natural sciences but in some more restricted area of scientific inquiry, and similarly in the fields of art, religion and social institutions. This drive to more and more intensive specialization is symbolized by the familiar organization of our universities into schools, of these schools into departments, and of these departments into a legion of individual courses whose proliferation signalizes the modern impulse to isolate specific problems for intensive study.

Such specialization is not only inevitable; it is productive of results which could not otherwise be obtained. For, on the creative side, it has always been the specialist who has succeeded in penetrating most deeply into the secrets of nature, who has been most sensitive to moral and religious values, and who has brought new beauty and new forms of social organization into being. Similarly, it has been the specialist in historical and systematic criticism whose interpretations of the course of human events and of mankind's various achievements have proved to be most illuminating. Thus it is to the specialists that we are indebted for all the specific creations, discoveries, interpretations and insights which, in combination, constitute the body of our cultural heritage. Whatever the dangers of specialization, a more synoptic view of reality, divorced from the positive contributions of the specialist, is sure to be empty and superficial. This is a truth which historians in search of encyclopedic wisdom and philosophers concerned with reality as a whole should never forget.

In general, however, we need today to be reminded rather of the peculiar and tragic danger which attends specialization in any field. This danger assumes many forms but reduces in essence to a loss of perspective issuing in parochial blindness and unjustifiable dogmatism. The world in which we live gives increasing evidence of intricate internal relationships suggesting an organic structure rather than an aggregate of unrelated parts, while human experience itself, however varied and diversified, takes on significance only in proportion as different insights and reactions interfuse to produce a unified knowledge and an integrated response. To the extent to which the specialist in any field loses sight of this fact and becomes preoccupied with creative, inventive or critical details, his own life suffers cultural impoverishment, his own labors run the risk of being misguided, and even his positive achievements lack larger significance until they are interpreted by someone else in a more catholic spirit. The narrow specialist is also inclined to be sentimental and dogmatic regarding subjects which he has not investigated. However learned and modest he may be in his own domain, his ignorance of other subjects leads him too often to insist upon the application of methods and criteria, cogent in his own speciality, to regions where they are inapplicable, and to ignore valid empirical evidence and judicious interpretations in fields other than his own. Witness the unconsidered rejection of religion by many contemporary scientists and the repudiation of established scientific theories by many theologians. The specialist, in short, limited as he is to a highly restricted subject-matter and technique, too often cuts himself off from many of the vital interests and achievements of mankind, loses a sense of more fundamental values and ultimate objectives, and lapses into a spurious and insolent self-sufficiency which is finally disastrous not only to his own well-being but to that of the society in which he lives.

Introduction

Our age, meanwhile, has been prone to a peculiar veneration for specialists, a veneration which expresses itself in uncritical acceptance not merely of what the specialist proclaims regarding his own speciality but also of his most dogmatic and uninformed pronouncements on every subject under heaven. Thus successful manufacturers and clerics have been heard with awe on matters of economic and governmental policy, about which they were patently ignorant, and famous scientists have been listened to as authorities on questions of religion and morals.

The dictator in the modern totalitarian state is, in a sense, the symbol of the common man's increasing revolt against the leadership of narrow-minded specialists. Repudiating the advice of experts in every field of major human interest, the modern dictator takes it upon himself to settle by fiat all the questions which have perplexed the finest minds of every age and to pronounce with divine authority what his followers shall accept in religion and art, science and social theory. Here all the positive achievements of valid specialization are lost and the worst dangers of a dogmatism issuing from ignorance are realized.

The world needs today, as seldom before, wise leadership; and true wisdom involves a comprehension of the parts in their relation to the larger whole. If the more limited and dogmatic of modern specialists, on the one hand, and the more arrogant and bigoted of modern dictators, on the other, be regarded as symptomatic of our modern cultural confusion, the urgent need for wise and informed leadership becomes dramatically evident. Too many of our leaders are lacking either in larger orientation or in specialized knowledge, or both. Wherever we turn we come upon men in positions of authority who are wordy demagogues or irresponsible theorists rather than statesmen; artistic faddists rather than creative artists of true vision; scientists who repudiate the validity of insights other than their own; narrow theologians and emotional evangelists who have lost contact with a living Deity and the vital needs of mankind; educators with no inkling of the nature and goal of true education; philosophers content to dismiss all vital philosophical questions as "meaningless," and historians unable wisely to interpret the "facts" that they discover or to make the past enlighten the present. No wonder that our culture, though infinitely superior to other cultures in specialized knowledge and techniques, is so lacking in spiritual vitality, so insensitive to the higher values and so madly determined to use its own achievements as instruments of self-destruction.

How may this situation be corrected? Most emphatically not by the abandonment of specialization; the stupidities of the dictator and the demagogue testify to the folly of this solution. Significant creation and discovery can take place only through mastery of specialized techniques applied to specific materials and problems. Even the historian and the philosopher, whose perspectives should by rights be the most synoptic of all, must themselves be specialists in their respective disciplines. They can, moreover, hope to avoid futile generalization only through cooperation with experts in specific fields, for synthesis which is not a rich fusion of concrete particulars is vacuous and idle. But, as we have seen, particulars divorced from a wider context are blind and meaningless. Hence the more diversified specialization becomes, the more essential it is that it be oriented, if not by the specialist himself, then by others in his community, to a frame of reference within which all partial insights can have their place and contribute to a cultural perspective. The potentially invaluable achievements of specialists, in short, can be made actually to promote human welfare only through an effective re-definition of man's true end and the enlightened re-discovery of our larger cultural heritage. The goal of all humanistic enterprise is the attainment of such wisdom.

Introduction xxxiii

5. My description of man's humanistic ideal as an "historico-philosophical synthesis" attributes to history and philosophy a unique place in any cultural program. This attribution is justifiable only if these disciplines are defined not narrowly, as the sole concern of professional historians and philosophers, but in a much more catholic sense, as the concern of all cultured individuals. History and philosophy, broadly conceived, are of vital import to man because they constitute the only possible ways in which the particular experiences of the race and of the individual can be interpreted in their relation to one another and to reality as a whole.

For the world in which we live is in essence a temporal process manifesting recurrent qualities and enduring structures and values. It consists of a series of individual events which follow one another in time and which stand in qualitative and quantitative relation to one another. In the language of philosophy, it exhibits both multiplicity and unity, both variety and similarity, both novelty and order. Hence, if reality is to be intelligible to us, its multiplicity, variety and novelty must be apprehended in terms of unity, similarity and order. This, in turn, is possible, only through the organization of our moment to moment sensory contacts with reality, and of our successive emotive and hedonic responses to it, in terms of temporal sequence and systematic generalization. Were reality a meaningless chaos, our experience would be equally meaningless and chaotic. The fact that human experience is, in varying degrees, intelligible indicates that reality is not a chaos but, at least in many respects, an orderly and meaningful cosmos. Its cosmic character, however, can be apprehended only through strenuous endeavor on our part, and this endeavor must take the form of cooperative reconstruction and interpretation. But there are two, and only two, basic modes of interpretation, the historical, in terms of temporal sequence, and the systematic, in terms of more enduring quality and structure. These, in turn, are mutually dependent, since temporal process is intelligible only by reference to recurrent patterns and ideal objectives, and since structural relations and timeless values can acquire significance for man only by being referred to the objective sequence of events and to the temporality of human experience. The temporal and the timeless are thus the two basic axes of objective reality, on the one hand, and of subjective experience, on the other; it is only by reference to these two axes that reality becomes intelligible and the human mind intelligent.

It has been the purpose of our analysis to demonstrate this truth. We have described the experience of an hypothetical being without memory, reason or imagination to emphasize man's crucial dependence upon these faculties; without them his experience would be mere sub-human atomistic awareness. The predicament of a fictitious solitary mind was envisaged to indicate man's profound indebtedness to social traditions and institutions; without the aid of his fellow-men the most brilliant and energetic genius could interpret his own experience and his complex environment only in the most fragmentary way. Mere social convention, however, will not suffice to render human life meaningful, for it can only preserve and transmit the cumulative achievements of the race; individual dignity and worth depend on individual initiative expressing itself in specialized creative and critical activity. The centrifugal tendency of specialization, finally, threatens to plunge society into a cultural chaos analogous to the primitive chaos of atomistic awareness, and this threat can be met only by a centripetal or cohesive force analogous, at the cultural level, to the uncritical synthesis of the solitary mind. Cultural, *i.e.,* historical and philosophical, synthesis, in a word, is imperative if society is to achieve spiritual unity and if men and women are to enjoy a rich and meaningful existence.

Introduction

As a matter of fact, each of the more developed specialized disciplines invoke, in one way or another, both the principles of interpretation which we have designated as the historical and the philosophical. Each discipline has not only evolved in time but betrays more or less awareness of the historical emergence of its own basic concepts and of the temporal character of its subject-matter. And each discipline is not only systematic in its methodology but, in proportion to its maturity as a discipline, is concerned to clarify its basic interpretative concepts and exploratory methods. Thus the social sciences, literary and artistic criticism, and the study of religion are all, in essence, both historical and systematic inquiries, and even the natural sciences, though primarily concerned with enduring structure, cannot ignore their own historical development or the temporal character of their subject-matter.[2] In this sense all competent specialists are necessarily both historians and philosophers.

Professional historians and philosophers, however, have a peculiar responsibility which only they can assume. They differ from other specialists in two essential ways, first, in having no distinctive subject-matter of their own, and, second, in possessing a unique and invaluable perspective. For the true subject-matter of the historian, considered in its widest scope, is the sum-total of past events, while the concern of the philosopher is reality as a whole and human experience in all its length and breadth. Other specialists investigate more restricted and overlapping areas of this same process and this same reality, and it is their peculiar function to delve deeply into these areas and to explore them with empirical immediacy. It is the duty of the professional historian and philosopher, in contrast, to interpret the achievements of these specialists more synoptically, the historian with prior emphasis on time, the philosopher with

---

[2] Professors Panofsky, Perry and Calhoun discuss the ways in which the natural sciences *differ* from the purer humanistic disciplines.

special concern for value and recurrent structure. When historians and philosophers bemoan the emergence of new specialized disciplines, such as psychology and the social sciences, as robbing them of part of their subject-matter, they seriously misconceive their prerogatives and duties. They should rather rejoice at the prospect of such cooperative assistance, for their own effectiveness as synoptic observers of a larger pattern depends essentially upon the minute exploration by others of more limited areas. The more competent these empirical and theoretical studies, the more assured will be the evidence and interpretations available to historians and philosophers alike.

Meanwhile both history and philosophy, regarded as synoptic disciplines, are fundamentally dependent on one another. The historian, in his survey of the past, must employ methods of investigation whose validity can be tested only by philosophical inquiry. Historical research involves the weighing of evidence according to certain criteria and the interpretation of this evidence in terms of basic principles and values; and the validity of these criteria, principles and values can be determined only by means of a philosophical critique. Philosophy, in turn, is equally dependent upon history. For, on the one hand, the reality whose abiding structure and pervasive values it is concerned to explore is a temporal and dynamic process, and the experiences of mankind whose significance it wishes to interpret are essentially temporal and purposive. Hence a philosophy which ignores or minimizes the importance of time and teleology condemns itself to the limbo of ultimately meaningless abstractions. Every philosopher, on the other hand, is inescapably a product of his own age and culture, and every philosophy is an historical phenomenon to be understood adequately only in its historical context. However essential its preoccupation with timeless verities, philosophy, like other disciplines, has evolved in time, and it is only through the study of its historical evolution that the significance of philosophical theories, ancient and modern, stand revealed. A philosopher who divorces himself from history, therefore, cuts himself off from his own cultural heritage and vitally impairs his own philosophical insights. In short, just as each of the more restricted disciplines must, to be truly effective, be both historical and philosophical in a more limited sense, so the more embracing disciplines of history and philosophy must be oriented to one another. The truly synoptic perspective is neither purely historical nor purely philosophical but both, in organic relation; the ideal cultural or humanistic outlook is historico-philosophical.

The task of historico-philosophical synthesis must, in the nature of the case, be unending. No one supposes that the labors of the specialist will ever be completed; while the human race endures, new works of art will continue to be created, new discoveries will be made and new social patterns will evolve in each successive generation. This means that historians and philosophers must return again and again to the task of relating an ever-changing present to an ever-extending past, and of interpreting the more inadequate and partial in terms of the more precise and comprehensive. This unending process will constitute a cultural advance, meanwhile, only if older insights are not lost in the enthusiasm for new discoveries and creations and only if man's earlier achievements are continually revitalized by new experiences and fresh perspectives.

The cultural objective, then, is an ideal which must ever elude final achievement by mortal man. The humanist can assert his humanity, however, through steadfast allegiance to this cultural ideal and through cooperative endeavor to approximate ever more closely to its adequate realization. And just because the humanist is temperamentally an individualist, it is of vital importance that he appreciate the need for widespread cooperation in this cultural enterprise.

The common man needs the assistance of the specialist and both, whether they realize it or not, need the expert guidance of the philosopher and the historian; but the philosopher and historian depend quite as much upon the specialist, and both are ultimately dependent upon social conventions and contact with the experiences and beliefs of the common man. To divorce the three higher levels of experience which we have been at pains to isolate for purposes of analysis would be to condemn society to sheer convention, the specialist to esoteric myopia, and the professional historian and philosopher to idle speculation. It is only through the fusion of these levels that we can hope to achieve, individually and collectively, contemplative wisdom, practical sagacity and human dignity.

The foregoing analysis is offered as a preliminary exploration of the humanistic ideal envisaged in one way or another by the authors contributing to this volume. Each essay subjects certain aspects of the humanistic enterprise to more intensive scrutiny. Professor Perry's emphasis on freedom as the prime requisite to human dignity, his analysis of its nature and conditions, and his appraisal of the several major disciplines in terms of this cultural criterion, is clearly integral to any definition of the humanistic attitude. Professor Calhoun's insistence on the need for commitment in all humanistic endeavor is equally pertinent. Freedom and commitment, autonomy and loyalty to objective values, thus emerge as the two most essential characteristics of humanistic activity. In his discussion of theology, Professor Calhoun also makes clear the limits of the humanistic enterprise regarded as man's attempt to enrich his experience through his own unaided efforts. The value of the cultural ideal is in no way impugned by an honest belief that salvation, whether social or individual, is possible only with the aid of a benefi-

Introduction

cent Deity and demands ultimate religious commitment on our part. These systematic studies are complemented by Professor Krey's historical survey of the rise and development of the cultural ideal in the Renaissance. Professors Panofsky and Chinard, in turn, consider more in detail the peculiar methods and problems of art and literary criticism, with special reference to the nature of their respective subjects, their relation to other disciplines, and their contributions to human culture. Each of these five essays, finally, deals, either explicitly or implicitly, with the requirements of a liberal education and considers the deficiencies of contemporary educational ventures. But the essays can be left to speak for themselves. If the volume as a whole helps to clarify some of the basic issues and perennial problems which every humanist must face, the authors will, I am confident, feel amply rewarded for their labors.

A DEFINITION OF THE HUMANITIES
By Ralph Barton Perry

A DEFINITION OF THE HUMANITIES

I

A CURSORY examination of the subject revealed the fact that the term "humanities" had no fixed meaning. Starting at scratch, namely, with *Webster's New International Dictionary,* I found that "humanity 3b usually in *pl.,* with *the*" means "the branches of polite learning, esp. the ancient classics; belles-lettres; sometimes, secular, as distinguished from theological, learning." Turning to a standard *Dictionary of Education and Instruction,*[1] I learned that the humanities consist of certain branches the study of which "has a tendency to *humanize* man," in opposition to the physical sciences, "which especially develop the intellectual faculties." From this same dictionary I learned that the humanities were embraced within what is called "liberal education," and that this, being "suited to the condition and wants of a freeman or a gentleman," was "contrasted with a *practical* education." Then, knowing that John Henry Newman is often quoted on the subject, I found that according to this authority liberal education was "intellectual culture," in which "the intellect, instead of being formed or sacrificed to some particular or accidental purpose, some specific trade or profession, or study or science, is disciplined for its own sake."[2]

Having proceeded thus far and discovered that "the humanities" signified, as one liked, either the secular vs. the theological, or the social and moral vs. the intellectual, or the intellectual vs. the practical, I came to the conclusion that where ambiguity and incoherence thus abounded I should have to make a definition for myself. Which is, of course,

[1] Henry Kiddle and A. J. Schem, 1881, pp. 168, 196.
[2] *The Idea of a University,* 1899, pp. 152, 165.

precisely the situation in which a philosopher finds himself most at home. No doubt those who arranged this program, and included a philosopher, reckoned with the speculative and not merely historical or descriptive aspects of the subject.

I define "the humanities," then, to embrace whatever influences conduce to freedom. "The humanities" is not to be employed as a mere class name for certain divisions of knowledge or parts of a scholastic curriculum, or for certain human institutions, activities and relationships, but to signify a certain condition of freedom which these may serve to create. The meaning of "the humanities" is relative to the meaning of that condition. The term "influence" implies that freedom in the sense of my definition is no inborn natural or metaphysical trait, but a possibility of human development which may or may not be realized through growth and interaction with the environment. The degree of its realization will depend on ancestral traits and the accidents of genius, but it lies within the range of those agencies by which men make men, or by which men make themselves, what they are.

But what is meant by freedom? Here again I can only state what for the purpose of this discussion I propose to mean by "freedom," disregarding the propriety of the term and admitting that there are other equally legitimate meanings. By freedom I mean enlightened choice. I mean the action in which habit, reflex or suggestion are superseded by an individual's fundamental judgments of good and evil; the action whose premises are explicit; the action which proceeds from personal reflection and integration. This, I take it, is substantially what Montaigne meant, when he described liberal education.

> Let the tutor make his pupil sift everything, and lodge nothing in his head upon simple authority and trust. Let not the principles of Aristotle be principles to him, any more than those of the Stoics and

Epicureans. Let this diversity of opinions be laid before him; he will choose, if he be able; if not, he will remain in doubt. *Only fools are sure and immovable.* . . . For if he embrace the opinions of Xenophon and Plato by his own reason, they will no longer be theirs, they will become his own. *Who follows another, follows nothing. He finds nothing, nay, he seeks nothing.* . . . *"We are not subjects of a king: let each one claim his own freedom."* . . . Truth and reason are common to every one, and no more belong to him who spoke them first than to him who speaks them after. . . . Bees pilfer from this flower and that, but afterwards make honey thereof which is all their own; it is no longer thyme and marjoram; so the pieces he borrows from others, he will transform and fuse to make of them a work that shall be absolutely his own, that is to say, his judgment. His education, his labour and study, tend to nothing else but to form that. . . . It is the understanding, said Epicharmus, that sees and hears, it is the understanding that improves everything, that orders everything, that acts, rules, and reigns: all other things are blind, and deaf, and without soul. Truly we render it abject and cowardly in not allowing it the liberty to do anything of itself. . . . The first lessons with which one should slake his understanding ought to be those which regulate his morals and his sense, which will teach him to know himself and how both to die well and to live well. *Among the liberal arts let us begin with that which makes us free.*[3]

By enlightened choice, I do not mean effective choice. For that I should prefer to reserve the term "liberty." Thus a man who chooses to roam abroad may be compelled to remain

---

[3] "Of the Education of Children," *The Essays of Michel de Montaigne,* translated and edited by Jacob Zeitlin, 1934, I, 131-2, 139. The citation is from Seneca, *Epistles,* xxxiii, 4: "Non sumus sub rege; sibi quisque se vindicet."

where he is, restrained by prison bars or lack of means. His choice may be enlightened, though he be deprived of the means of execution. I recognize the fact that freedom and liberty interact upon one another. External compulsion sets limits to choice, and conditions its degree of enlightenment. But unless the prisoner *chooses* to roam abroad his imprisonment does not deprive him of liberty—there is no clash between his will and his circumstances. Choice determines whether compulsion shall be gladly accepted, or turned to good use, or circumvented, or helplessly resented. Liberty has to do with the action of circumstance upon the man, freedom with a man's action on circumstance.

The extent to which a man is free, that is, exercises enlightened choice, depends in the first place upon the extent to which he is aware of the possibilities. In so far as a man is ignorant of what there is to choose, alternatives are eliminated not by rejection but by accident. Freedom is proportional to the range of options. The first condition of freedom, then, is "learning." To promote freedom it is necessary to enlarge the span of man's consciousness by acquainting him both with the world and with "the best that has been known and thought in the world."[4] The free man must enjoy possession of his natural, intellectual and moral inheritance.

The principle of freedom argues for breadth rather than concentration of knowledge, and for subject-matter rather than method. In 1882, at the age of twenty-three, Bergson addressed the pupils of the lycée at Angers as follows:

> Every one of us should begin, as mankind began, with the noble yet simple-minded ambition to know everything.... Here precisely is what distinguishes intellect from instinct and man from beast. The inferiority of the animal lies entirely in this—that it is

---

[4] "The Function of Criticism," *Essays in Criticism* (*The Works of Matthew Arnold*, 1902, III), p. 20.

a specialist. It does one thing to admiration; it can do nothing else.[5]

The distinction between content and method has created a false antithesis between learning and *training*. The mind is not a weapon to be sharpened or a muscle to be strengthened. Every man's experience confirms the consensus of the experts in rejecting the convenient idea of a "formal training" that is transferable at will from one subject to another, as scissors will cut all kinds of cloth, or a strong muscle move all kinds of objects. There is such a thing as intellectual skill, but there are as many skills as there are types of subject-matter. The intellect takes its subject-matter along with its skill, or leaves its skill behind with the old subject-matter. There is no form of intellectual incapacity more flagrant in modern times than that which results from the assumption that a man who has sharpened his wits on mathematics can therefore think soundly about economics, or that a trained philologist is *eo ipso* an expert in politics. It will be noted that men who have devoted their lives to physics or biology are likely to acquire a naturalistic philosophy; or, if not, to become indifferent theologians. It is valid to distinguish between skill and method, and to say that the latter can be generalized and extended to a new subject-matter. But this is possible only when the method itself is consciously reflected upon—when, in short, it becomes a subject-matter.[6] In the case of the intellect the instrumental metaphor is profoundly misleading. The intellect is not itself an instrument, but it uses instruments; and in order to use them it must acquire and possess them. The metaphor of a garden, though this also is capable of abuse, is more trustworthy; and in order that a

[5] Quoted in A. Ruhe and N. M. Paul, *Henri Bergson. An Account of His Life and Philosophy*, 1914, pp. 4, 5.
[6] For an authoritative discussion of this question of "formal training," cf. Guy M. Whipple, "The Transfer of Training," *Twenty-seventh Yearbook of the National Society for the Study of Education*, Part II, 1928.

garden shall be cultivated, it requires not only to be ploughed but to be fertilized and planted.

But if we are to hold firmly to our principle of freedom, it is evident that mere volume of content will not suffice. Content must be so diversified as to represent the major alternatives of thought; and given the limited capacity of the mind, this implies that the parts of knowledge shall be subsumed under principles. Even were the mind of cosmic dimensions this would still be desirable, for the greater part of knowledge is relevant to choice only in *general* terms. Some few specific items of fact are illuminating to choice at the point of application, where thought is about to be translated into action, and where the major choices have already been made. For the most part facts bear on life only through the moral which they point. For reasons both of economy and of relevance the knowledge of principles takes precedence of the knowledge of particulars.

Learning, in the liberal sense, then, is a wide awareness of the laws and natures of the known world, and of the procedures of knowledge; it provides the map and compass with which the latest man can chart his own course within those seas and continents that have been discovered region upon region by all the voyagers that have gone before.

A second condition of enlightened choice is imagination. While learning in the usual intellectual sense provides the mind with alternatives that are held for true, imagination enables the mind to entertain mere possibilities of truth. It plays wantonly with the doubtful, the improbable and the incredible. It is of the essence of fancy that it should be free. Imagination is the agency by which the human mind looks beyond every self-imposed limitation, conscious or unconscious; it is the chief antidote to habit; it recognizes no impossibility within the elastic power of invention. Here again, as in the case of the intellect, it is a mistake to suppose that there is a faculty which can be sharpened like a tool or strengthened like a muscle. But the imagination, like the intellect, can be fed; or provided with "a garden of bright images," wherein to wander.[7]

But options are not options until they appeal to feeling and will. To be an alternative of choice implies that an idea shall move and excite, or shall be invested with that attractiveness which it is now customary to call "value." The human faculty by which values are envisaged and multiplied so that a man out of a wealth of goods may be a chooser of the best, may be called sympathy. This means that truths shall be acquired together with the passion for their truthfulness, the force of their evidence, and the joy of their contemplation; art together with the enjoyment of its beauty; history with solicitude for the rising and declining fortunes of man; discovery with the relish of adventure; enterprise with the aspiration which impels men to its pursuit. Knowing through sympathy the taste of the diverse satisfactions which life affords, one may be said to have chosen wittingly, and not merely by default.

There are four chief hindrances to the enlargement of man's range of values. The first of these is simple apathy. The second is the individual's preoccupation with his own subjectivity. A fellow-creature is a means or an obstacle to one's own preëxisting ends—a value, positive or negative, in terms of what one already desires for oneself. Viewing him in this light one tends to overlook that which is good to *him*—the object of *his* liking or aspiration. In the glaring light of one's own felt interests, the innumerable interests all about—the hopes and fears and joys and sorrows of other men—are invisible. One thus lives in a narrow province, embracing only a minute fraction of the values of the larger world. The only remedy for this blindness is sympathy—the

---

[7] Ernest Bramah, *Kai Lung's Golden Hours*, 1922, p. 258.

power of feeling to penetrate to the centers of other men and share the outlook of *their* emotional life.

The third hindrance to the enlargement of the field of values is preoccupation with the means to a present end. This limitation may be imposed by circumstance. A man who is in peril of his life can choose only among the means of self-preservation. When the struggle for existence is hard and relentless, the options are restricted to food, drink and shelter. When the enemy is present in arms and a man's fighting blood is aroused, he has no choice but the manner of dealing or receiving blows. A similar impoverishment results from the hasty adoption of an end, or from yielding to suggestion, or from a headlong impetuousness, or from an intensity of absorption. An end may usurp control without having been deliberately preferred, and all choices from thenceforth be limited to its means. The maximum of freedom requires that there shall be at least moments of life in which a man freely chooses that ultimate goal which prescribes the chain of subordinate choices with which the greater part of his life is necessarily concerned. To exercise this faculty of ultimate choice requires a discriminating taste, and a familiarity with what life has to "offer." It implies detachment from the importunity of appetite, from sectarian zeal, the pressure of need, the passion of the mob, the slavish adherence to custom and vogue, or any other force that deadens the heart to wide tracts of the realm of values.

A fourth force which works perpetually to narrow the range of values is the tendency of means to usurp the place of ends. A man who leaves his country on account of religious persecution and settles in the wilderness in order to worship God finds that in order to worship God he must live, and that in order to live he must subjugate the wilderness. In time he is likely to forget God, and devote himself with his whole heart to the acquisition of material goods. Christmas celebrates the spirit of giving, but the business of giving tends to degenerate into the discharge of obligations or the tying and untying of bits of string. Such a change is not always a degradation of values, but there is, in any case, an oblivion of values and a reduction of alternatives.

Learning, imagination and sympathy constitute the conditions of that freedom which I have defined as the norm by which to judge whether any study or other occasion of experience is or is not a "humanity." The propriety of the name itself rests on the assumption that this norm is peculiarly concerned with man. And the term "man" here means the natural man: not the physical man in any restricted sense, but the actual man, of metaphysics as well as physics—man as he springs from his biological ancestry or from the creative act of God, rather than any monster or celestial being that may by the blight of atavism or the grace of God be substituted for him. But the reference is not to man's characteristics, but to his characteristic perfection. The reference to man in the context of the so-called "humanities" is, then, not descriptive or apologetic, but eulogistic; not "human—all too human," or "only human," but human in the sense in which one deems it highest praise to be called "a man." It is possible so to conceive man as either to exalt or debase him. Both of these ways of conceiving him are in accordance with the facts: man is, in fact, both respectable and disreputable, honorable and contemptible. I use the term "dignity" to signify that characteristic which is *worthy* of a man—which distinguishes him either as the highest phase of natural evolution or as the masterpiece of creation; and at the same time to imply that self-feeling and social relations shall be impregnated with the esteem which this characteristic deserves.

That man owes his dignity to the possession of freedom happily requires little argument. His dignity may be small, great, or even non-existent: but what dignity he has, or would have if he had any, lies in the capacity of the individual to choose for himself.

> ... the will is free;
> Strong is the soul, and wise, and beautiful;
> The seeds of godlike power are in us still;
> Gods are we, bards, saints, heroes, if we will!⁸

Or, to protect myself against the charge of echoing Victorian piety, let me pass from Matthew Arnold to Theodore Dreiser:

> We are here, I take it, not merely to moon and vegetate, but to do a little thinking about this state in which we find ourselves. It is perfectly legitimate, all priests and theories and philosophies to the contrary notwithstanding, to go back, in so far as we may, to the primary sources of thought, *i.e.*, the visible scene, the actions and thoughts of people, the movements of nature and its chemical and physical subtleties, in order to draw original and radical conclusions for ourselves. The great business of an individual, if he has any time after struggling for life and a reasonable amount of entertainment or sensory satiation, should be this very thing. A man, if he can, should question the things that he sees—not some things, but everything—stand, as it were, in the center of this whirling storm of contradiction which we know as life, and ask of it its source and its import.⁹

Christianity teaches that man is the end of creation and that his supremacy over other creatures lies in his freedom; a capacity so exalted that it is worth the price of its misuse, and the tragic consequences of sin. It is in respect of his freedom that a man is the image of his Creator. Or, approached from below, man emerges upon that level beyond tropism, reflex and instinct, in which life assumes the form of volition and

---

⁸ Matthew Arnold, "Written in Emerson's Essays," *Poems*, 1881, I, 6.
⁹ "Life, Art and America," *The Seven Arts*, February 1917, p. 369.

reason. In the development of man himself, civilized man, and the élite within a civilized society, are marked by their emancipation in greater or less degree from custom and blind impulsions.

Freedom constitutes the dignity of man, *qua* man. It is both a dignity and a generic attribute. Though it may be, and is, possessed in varying degrees, it is not the exclusive prerogative of any individual or race or class. The cultivation of freedom does not set a man apart from his fellows but implies a sense of universal kinship. The pride which it justifies is a common pride. And since freedom is the generic attribute its exercise is the generic vocation. It is the high calling of every man, distinct from those several callings through which men exchange services and take their allotted places in the division of labor. There is a passage in Huxley's famous address "On the Educational Value of the Natural History Sciences," in which the author stresses "the practical value of physiological instruction," and deplores the general ignorance among men of "the conditions of the existence they prize so highly":

> I dare venture to assert that, with the exception of those of my hearers who may chance to have received a medical education, there is not one who could tell me what is the meaning and use of an act which he performs a score of times every minute, and whose suspension would involve his immediate death;—I mean the act of breathing.[10]

But men breathe very successfully without a knowledge of physiology. Indeed no procedure would be better calculated to produce asphyxiation than the attempt to breathe physiologically. And when a man has respiratory difficulties he will, if he is wise, consult a physician rather than a medical textbook. It is humanly important that somebody should

[10] Thomas Huxley, *Lay Sermons, Addresses, and Reviews*, 1874, p. 89.

understand the physiology of breathing, but it is neither possible nor desirable that everybody should possess that understanding. The mass of mankind will obtain the services of the medical expert in exchange for some like expertness of their own. They do not need this medical understanding, but only its results. What they do need—what every man needs—is such illumination as shall enable him to judge the importance of health, or to "prize" that existence of which health and respiration are the conditions. Of special skills no man needs more than one, or at most very few. The so-called "useful arts" are either possessed by all men as a part of their original endowment of reflexes, or can be borrowed. That which every man needs to possess in his own right is what will minister to his exercise of choice. I can utilize the enlightenment of others once my choice is made; but I cannot choose by any light that does not shine within the chamber of my own consciousness.

There is, to be sure, an alternative theory of human dignity. Those from Plato to Hegel who stress the organic character of the state have seemed to affirm that men are ennobled by their participation in a greater collective being or social totality, and that for the mass of mankind the highest form of life is to be found in that loyalty or discipline which accepts the judgment of authority. But the judgment of authority is exercised by men. The political organism does not exercise judgment in its corporate capacity, but only through the minds of certain privileged members. The ruler is a man like other men, who examines the situation, faces alternatives, consults advisers, and eventually makes decisions. There is, I think, no doubt, even in the minds of totalitarians, that the man who makes decisions is a more developed human being, a more adequate instance of what a man at his best can be, than those who merely accept and follow his decisions. To prevent this degradation of the remainder to the rôle of passive acquiescence, totalitarians resort to one or both of two expedients: the fiction that the decision of the ruler is the "real" will of his followers, regardless of what they may consciously think or feel; and the use of propaganda to engender a blind fidelity which automatically adopts the decision of the ruler whatever it be, and merely because it is his. In neither case does the follower exercise the function of free choice after the manner of the ruler. There is no difference among social philosophies as to the highest state of man, but only as to whether this state shall be considered a privilege reserved for a few, or an opportunity extended to all.

I take it, then, that the dignity of man lies in his freedom. There remains a last and supervening quality which belongs to the domain of manners. There is no name for this quality, whether it be called refinement, courtesy, gentility, elegance, graciousness or polish, which does not impoverish its meaning. There is an outward aspect of that inner state which we have called freedom. There is a mode of bearing and of address that becomes a man in the dignitative sense. There is a *noblesse oblige* for every man, by virtue of his human birth and human calling. "The greater man, the greater courtesy."[11] The outward manner will express an inner pride and an inner humility—a humble sense of falling short of that high level to which one proudly aspires. It will include a deference to fellow-man, and an acknowledgment of the equal finality of his values. It will be gentle and forbearing. It will be quick to sense another's inward thoughts and feelings and so promote a genuine reciprocity of intercourse. It constitutes that attitude of man to man which is appropriate to a society of men in which men are indeed men. If a man be blessed with a tongue and a native wit, his liberality of mind will provide him resources, so that he will be capable

---

[11] Tennyson, "Idylls of the King. The Last Tournament," *The Works of Alfred Lord Tennyson*, 1889, p. 453.

of conversation. If he have a further gift of linguistic form, he may converse well. For these and other outward signs of inner freedom, in their composite flavor, there is no name. Seeking a word that is colorless enough to lend itself to a given meaning, I shall call it civility.

Here, then, is that freedom, or exercise of enlightened choice, by which I define that which is variously called "humane," "humanity," "humanistic," "humanism," or "liberal culture." Its specifications are: learning, imagination, sympathy, dignity and civility. You may recognize them by their opposites. The man who lacks freedom is ignorant, narrow, indoctrinated or dogmatic, through lack of learning; literal-minded, pedantic, habituated or vulgar, through lack of imagination; insensible, apathetic, prejudiced, censorious, opportunistic, sordid or self-absorbed, through lack of sympathy; base, ascetic, trivial, or snobbish, through lack of dignity; dull, boorish or brutal, through lack of civility.

II

We may now turn to history, and distinguish the essential meaning of humanity from its accidental embodiments and associations. The term and its variants came into vogue in the fifteenth century to designate the educational ideal inspired by the Renaissance and by the Italian "Revival of Letters" of the preceding century. This ideal was both cause and effect of an interest in antiquity. It was reminiscent of the *humanitas* of Cicero, and of its famous formulation by Aulus Gellius in the second century A.D.[12] It signified the emancipation of

---

[12] "Those who have spoken Latin and have used the language correctly do not give to the word *humanitas* the meaning which it is commonly thought to have, namely, what the Greeks called φιλανθρωπία, signifying a kind of friendly spirit and good-feeling towards all men without distinction; but they gave to *humanitas* about the force of the Greek παιδεία; that is, what we call *eruditionem institutionemque in bonas artes,* or 'education and training in the liberal arts.' Those who earnestly desire and seek after these are most highly humanized. For the pursuit of that kind of knowledge, and the training given by it, have been granted to man

the human faculties from the restraints of religious zeal, preoccupation or authority; the reinstatement of natural and secular values after their disparagement by the cult of otherworldliness, the illumination of the darkness of ignorance, the breaking of the bonds of habit, and everywhere a passage beyond the narrow circle and rigid hierarchy of intermediaries to original and authentic sources in human experience. It was conditioned by leisure and wealth. Together with political ambition, economic mobility, voyages of discovery, invention, and the flowering of art and literature, it was one of many parallel manifestations of self-reliant individualism and the incidence of genius.

In its earliest impulse and first inspired utterances humanism was thus a cult of freedom. It awakened in men a sense of their high calling, not through salvation, but through their intrinsic faculties and heritage of the past. Humanism sought not only to stir this sense of vocation, but to fulfill it, through the exercise of faculty and the appropriation of inheritance. Humanism did not oppose religion, or deny the superiority of religious to secular values;[18] nor did it slight the authority of the state. It sought to make room for the rights of personality within a religious and political frame. If it collided with church and state it was only where these were harshly repressive: it negated only their negations. In its own inner nature it was positive and not negative. Thus its impulse was not to oppose one form of learning to another, but to promote all learning, provided only that it *was* learning, and not merely a rudimentary, shallow or

alone of all the animals, and for that reason it is termed *humanitas,* or 'humanity.'" (*The Attic Nights of Aulus Gellius,* English translation by John C. Rolfe, Loeb Classical Library, 1927, II, 457.)

[18] "Christianity and Humanism were the two coordinate factors necessary to the development of complete manhood." (W. H. Woodward, *Vittorino da Feltre and other Humanist Educators,* 1897, p. 67.) cf. also "Lionardo D'Arezzo Concerning the Study of Literature—A Letter Addressed to the Illustrious Lady, Baptista Malatesta," in *ibid.,* p. 127.

dogmatic belief. "Europe owes to humanism," says Sir Richard Jebb, "the diffusion of a new spirit, the initiation of forces hostile to obscurantism, pedantry and superstition, forces making for intellectual light, for the advance of knowledge in every field."[14] The study of the Greek and Latin literatures served this purpose of learning in a double capacity. Their study was itself a form of learning, and they contained the learning of antiquity. With the early humanists these two parts of classical learning formed one indivisible whole. Men enthusiastically pursued those linguistic and historical studies by which they gained access to a store of wisdom which they enthusiastically appropriated.

But there was no disposition to study the ancient literatures exclusively. The early humanistic leaders were remarkable for the broad inclusiveness of their conception of liberal studies. Pietro Vergerius (1370-1445), whose *De ingenuis moribus et liberalibus studiis* is perhaps the greatest of all the early humanistic treatises in the field of education, recommended a curriculum which embraced history, moral philosophy, eloquence, grammar, composition, disputation, music, poetry, arithmetic, geometry, astronomy and nature study.[15] Vittorino da Feltre, who from 1425 to 1446 conducted at Mantua a kind of progressive school called "The Pleasant House," taught mathematics and science as well as the classics.[16] Lionardo D'Arezzo, like Vergerius, placed history first—for an "illustrious lady," to be sure. Both Vergerius and Aeneas Piccolomini placed philosophy before literature.[17]

That there was, indeed, a certain promiscuity and reckless abandon in this zeal for learning appears in Rabelais, in Gargantua's advice to Pantagruel. After recommending the mastery of all languages and adding history, geometry, arith-

[14] *Humanism in Education,* the Romanes Lecture, 1899, p. 15.
[15] W. H. Woodward, *op. cit.,* pp. 106-8.
[16] Jebb, *op. cit.,* pp. 17-20.
[17] W. H. Woodward, *op. cit,* pp. 106, 136-58.

A Definition of the Humanities

metic, music, astronomy and civil law, he comes to natural science:

> As for knowledge of the works of Nature, I would have thee devote thyself to them so that there may be no sea, river, or spring of which thou knowest not the fishes; all the birds of the air, all the trees, forest or orchard, all the herbs of the field, all the metals hid in the bowels of the earth, all the precious stones of the East and the South, let nothing be unknown to thee.
>
> Then turn again with diligence to the books of the Greek physicians, and the Arabs, and the Latin, without despising the Talmudists and the Cabalists; and by frequent dissections acquire a perfect knowledge of the other world, which is Man. . . . In brief, let me see thee an abyss and bottomless pit of knowledge.[18]

But there was, none the less, a limiting principle. For learning, being conjoined with imagination and feeling, was conceived as affording taste and wisdom rather than mere erudition. "The enthusiasm and the versatile energy which animated the Italian Renaissance for two centuries," writes Jebb in his famous Romanes Lecture, "sprang from a deep and earnest conviction that the recovered literatures were not only models of style, but treasure-houses of wisdom, guides of life, witnesses to a civilisation higher than any which could then be found upon the earth."[19] The recovered literatures were *literature,* and were apprehended as such. They possessed artistic form and were products of the creative imagination. They contained an order of values. Lionardo D'Arezzo speaks of "the peculiar affinity of rhythm and metre to our emotions and our intelligence."[20] Vergerius says:

---

[18] Quoted by Robert H. Quick, *Essays on Educational Reformers,* revised edition, 1890, pp. 68-9.
[19] Sir Richard Jebb, *op. cit.,* pp. 7-8.
[20] W. H. Woodward, *op. cit.,* p. 130.

Literature indeed exhibits not facts alone, but thoughts, and their expression. Provided such thoughts be worthy, and worthily expressed, we feel assured that they will not die: although I do not think that thoughts without style will be likely to attract much notice or secure a sure survival. What greater charm can life offer than this power of making the past, the present, and even the future, our own by means of literature?[21]

To grasp "the image of Antiquity in its strength and beauty"[22] required a sympathetic, and not a merely intellectual, appropriation of the past. Their study was pursued for the sake of a practical and not a merely theoretical end —practical in the sense of ministering to life. They were thought to reveal the good life, in order that a man might choose the best and conduct himself accordingly; and in order that by such enlightened self-regulation he might prove himself eminently a man. "We call those studies *liberal*," said Vergerius, "which are worthy of a free man; those studies by which we attain and practise virtue and wisdom; that education which calls forth, trains and develops those highest gifts of body and of mind which ennoble men, and which are rightly judged to rank next in dignity to virtue only. For to a vulgar temper gain and pleasure are the one aim of existence, to a lofty nature, moral worth and fame."[23]

Nor was the purpose of humanistic studies realized until a man had so far assimilated them to character and personality as to give them appropriate expression in manners and in social intercourse. When in 1515 Pope Leo X authorized the printing of a manuscript of Tacitus, he said of humanistic studies:

[21] W. H. Woodward, *op. cit.*, p. 105.
[22] John Burnet, *Essays and Addresses*, 1929, p. 36.
[23] W. H. Woodward, *op. cit.*, p. 102.

A Definition of the Humanities

> We have been accustomed, even from our early years, to think that nothing more excellent or more useful has been given by the Creator to mankind, if we except only the knowledge and true worship of Himself, than these studies, which not only lead to the ornament and guidance of human life, but are applicable and useful to every particular situation; in adversity consolatory, in prosperity pleasing and honourable; insomuch, that without them we should be deprived of all the grace of life and all the polish of social intercourse.[24]

A classic expression of this indivisibility of the humanistic ideal—of rounded learning, touched with feeling and imagination, conceived as worthy of a man, qualifying the individual to participate in the affairs of the world, and appropriately expressed in the outward forms of personal bearing and courtesy of manner—is Baldassar Castiglione's book of *The Courtier*.

> Our Courtier should therefore be circumspect in his every Undertaking; and Prudence attend whatever he says or acts: Nor should he think it enough that his Parts and Qualities be extraordinary, but ought so to regulate his Life, that all be agreeable to such Parts, and he throughout consistent with himself; whereby all his Excellencies may seem but the Parts of one whole, and every Action of his the Result and Compound of every Virtue, agreeably to the Description the Stoicks give us of a wise Man: For tho' whatever we do has in it some one predominant Virtue; yet are all so link'd that they respect the same End, and may all be made subservient, and applied to every Purpose.
>
> A wise Man therefore should know how to apply them, and by a proper Comparison, and as it were

---
[24] Quoted by Sir Richard Jebb, *op. cit.*, pp. 8-9.

Contrast, make one serve to the setting off another; like skilful Painters, who with Shadows sustain the Lights of a Relievo; as with Lights they throw back the Shadows on a Plane; so distributing their Colours, that each has its Beauty from its Opposition to the other, and so disposing their Attitudes, that by their Diversity they may assist each other in producing that Effect which the Artist intends them. Thus Courtesy is highly engaging in the Gentlemen of the Camp: and as their Modesty recommends their Courage, their Courage adds a Lustre to their Modesty. So likewise when our Words are few, but our Actions considerable; and of these, great as they are, we forbear to boast, and in a handsome Manner dissemble them; here one Virtue sets off another: and the very same it is with every Qualification that adorns us.[25]

Such is the humanism of the Renaissance in its universality as a cult of freedom, capable of being transferred to any time or place. With these universal characters were associated certain accidental characters which reflected its peculiar historical and local conditions; and in so far as it was identified with these, it was incapable of being transferred to other times and places without the violation of its universal characters.

It was retrospective. It arose as a reaction against the comparative ignorance of its own age, and found its inspiration, its models, its sources and even its content in the past. But pastness is no part of the essential meaning of humanism. If the Greeks, for example, were humanists it was not because they *revived,* but because they *created*. It is perfectly consistent with humanism that its ideal should be identified with contemporary life, or that it should be accompanied by the sense of a darker past succeeded by a brighter present.

[25] Conte Baldassar Castiglione, *The Courtier,* London, 1727, pp. 116-17.

A Definition of the Humanities

Transferred to the modern age a retrospective humanism can only result in a cult of the past as past, or in an enslaving traditionalism.

It was an historical accident, furthermore, that the past for which the Italian humanists of the fourteenth and fifteenth centuries felt a just reverence was the period of Graeco-Roman civilization. This was *their* past, in a double sense. It was to them the *immediate* past, and they were linked with it by cultural continuity; while Latin literature was at the same time their *national* literature, and Latin language their ancestral tongue, as well as the accepted language of the learned world. Roman culture had been fed by Greek, and to revive the Greek literature and language was only to follow the river to its source. But what Latin and Greek meant to the Italian humanists they can never mean again to any other time or place. To other ages they must be deader languages, from a remoter and more alien past. Greek and Latin literature, together with their linguistic and archaeological accessories, form no part of the definition of humanism in the universal sense. Their intrinsic value will give them a high place in every humanistic program, but their *unique* claims are relative to the age of the Renaissance, and this uniqueness cannot be asserted elsewhere without violence to that very liberality and livingness of which in the Renaissance they were the supremely fitting vehicle.

The meaning of humanism at the time of the Renaissance was relative to the existing *corpus* of human knowledge. In principle it meant the whole of learning, but in practice it meant so much of learning as was then possessed, being for the most part bequeathed by the ancients. This limited attainment of the times embraced a little science, a little modern literature, a little history, politics and economics: a little, but judged by later standards, not much. To convert this historical accident into the essence of humanism means that all subsequent increments or divisions of learning must fall outside and be disparaged. Whereas the spirit of humanism joyfully acclaims every extension of the area of knowledge, every new insight or creation of human genius, its letter excludes them.

The humanism of the Renaissance was also relative to the *doctrine* of antiquity, because it knew no other. Greek and Latin thought was, broadly speaking, rationalistic and teleological. It trusted intellectual intuition where modern thought would resort to sense perception; it found fixed principles where modern thought would find hypotheses, assumptions or probabilities; it found purpose in nature where modern thought would find mechanism. It is no part of the essential meaning of humanism to prescribe what the truth shall be, or what shall be its evidence. On the contrary, the spirit of humanism is open-minded and hospitable—curious, rich and varied in content and sceptical of all forms of crystallized and exclusive thought. In so far as humanism is identified with the intellectual content and method of antiquity it is indoctrinated in advance. Instead of being a cult of freedom it is a cult of dogma.

Finally, humanism was, in the particular time and place of its origin, a luxury and a privilege. It was a product of growing and concentrated wealth, and the special affair of princes and dignitaries. It required patronage and privilege, and was associated with class distinctions. But this, again, is no part of the essential meaning of humanism, as was proved by the more popular form which it assumed when transplanted to Germany and to England.[26] Humanism testifies to the eminence of man over the rest of creation, rather than to the eminence of certain species of men over others. It sets a high goal of perfection which only well-endowed men can hope to attain; it admires genius, and encourages

---

[26] cf. C. S. Parker, "On the History of Classical Education," in F. W. Farrar, *Essays on a Liberal Education*, 1868, pp. 27, 44 ff.

men to seek distinction. But to identify humanism with the exclusive attainment of a preferred class is a betrayal of its respect for the universal man.

The same is to be said of the humanistic code of manners. This was, through the accidents of origin, the code of the gentleman and the courtier. It was associated with gentility, with elegance, and with the politeness of that class which in the social hierarchy of the time determined the mode of fashion. But this was a local variant of its fundamental theme—that a man should in his outward bearing conduct himself as befitted a man who was truly a man living among men who were truly men. The essential civility of humanism is capable of being transferred from monarchies to republics, from court to market-place, from rich to poor; and there is nothing of its flavor that can be lost by its wide diffusion.

Never has humanism's essential code been more clearly distinguished from its accidental forms than in Bergson's address on "Good Manners," delivered at Clermont-Ferrand in 1885:

> Whereas the self-confident man annoys us by his determination to impose on everyone his own good opinion of himself, we are attracted by those who anxiously await from us that favourable verdict on their worth which we are willing to give. A well-timed compliment, a well-deserved eulogy, may produce in these delicate souls the effect of a sudden gleam of sunlight on a dreary landscape. . . . It takes up its dwelling in the soul and gives it warmth and support, inspiring that self-confidence which is the condition of joy, bringing hope into the present and offering an earnest of success to come. . . . Who among us, even the strongest and best equipped for the battle of life, has not known at times the pain of wounded self-respect, and felt as though the springs of the action he was about to

undertake were broken within him . . . while at other times he was uplifted in joy and a sense of harmony overflowed him, because the right word spoken in a happy hour reached that profound interior chord which can vibrate only when all the powers of life thrill in unison. It is some such word that we should know how and when to speak; therein lie the heart's good manners—the good manners that are a virtue. . . . Education, while it increases that mental flexibility which is a quality dominant in the man of the world, enables the best among us to acquire knowledge of the hearts of men, whereby kindliness is rendered skilful and becomes the good manners of the heart. This our forefathers recognized when they termed the studies of the later years of school life the humanities.[27]

III

The later history of the humanistic idea reveals the confusion due to the substitution of the accident for the essence, the letter for the spirit. Through this confusion humanism has fought unnecessary battles, in which it has in reality been at war with itself. Humanism has opposed itself to science, to humanitarianism, to democracy, to romanticism and to modernism. This is a formidable array of opponents, all of whom are in reality friends—enemies by accident and by letter, friends in essence and in spirit.

It was an historical accident that the humanism of the Renaissance neglected science. It arose before modern science was fully developed, and before its great destiny was revealed to the European mind. Such science as there was took its proportionate place in the humanistic program. To the early humanist pure science—that is, the knowledge of the fundamental constitution and laws of nature—was recognized as a

---

[27] A. Ruhe and N. M. Paul, *Henri Bergson. An Account of His Life and Philosophy*, 1914, pp. 12-14.

A Definition of the Humanities

triumph of human genius and as part of the hereditary treasure of wisdom. The modest proportions of science itself, the emphasis on the studies accessory to literature, and the hardening of traditional bias, placed humanism in a false position of jealousy and enmity toward the most momentous cultural development of modern Europe. A more universal and flexible humanism would have extolled the glory of science and claimed it as its own.

Similarly, it is no part of the meaning of humanism to narrow the range of human sympathies. It is not difficult to see how such a misunderstanding arose. At the time of the Renaissance the first enemy was ignorance, and the second was dogma and superstition. These last were associated in men's minds with the church, with divinity and theology as distinguished from secular literature, and with the sacred as distinguished from the profane. The simple Christian cult of brotherly love was prejudiced by this association. The emphasis of the Revival of Letters, furthermore, was on the cultural values of art and knowledge; or, in the domain of morals, on the pagan virtues of perfection, rather than on the Christian virtues of compassion and charity. And emphasis developed into exclusion; until in our own day a school of criticism which calls itself "Humanism," and which claims descent from the Renaissance and from antiquity, has accepted the suffering of mankind as an irremediable fatality, or as no-evil when judged from the higher standpoint of philosophical emancipation.[28] But it is no part of the essential meaning of humanism that it should be pagan or Thomist. Humanism is bound to oppose any exclusion of cultural values, or degradation of human destiny; and may justly suspect humanitarianism of an emphasis on needs rather than on ideal possibilities, and on pity rather than on admiration. But a true humanism

---

[28] I refer, of course, to the school of Irving Babbitt, Paul Elmer More, etc. Cf. Norman Foerster, *Toward Standards*, 1928, Chap. v; and Robert Shafer, *Paul Elmer More and American Criticism*, 1935, p. 212 and *passim*.

will not harden the heart. It will broaden its range of feeling to embrace the joys and sorrows of aggregate mankind. It will acknowledge the right of every man to the best, within the flexible limits of capacity, and will see that the first step towards this attainment by unfortunate men is to bind up their wounds and give them bread.

The antithesis of humanism to humanitarianism is, then, a false antithesis. The same can be said of its antithesis to democracy. Equalitarianism tends to a levelling down, rather than a levelling up, and to a substitution of vulgar or average attainment for ideal goods. Therefore humanism will be a vigilant critic, seeking to protect democracy against its own besetting sins. But the value of exclusiveness is not a humanistic value. The association of humanism with privilege, with airs of superiority, with the gratifying sense of belonging to a small élite, has grown from the accidents of its origin, and has nothing to do with the essence of its meaning. The true humanist should welcome the spread of his gospel, providing only that the salt shall not lose its savor. He should covet for every man that freedom which constitutes the dignity of man, and should deplore every impediment, necessary or remediable, which stands in the way of its universal attainment.

Romanticism has two meanings. In the primary sense it means a hospitable recognition of the great diversity of human values. It seeks out the inner lives of remote or alien men, encourages them to speak for themselves, and listens to them with deference. It credits feeling, and especially aesthetic feeling and the inspiration of creative genius, with a kind of truth. The secondary sense of romanticism is an outgrowth of the first, as despotism is an outgrowth of anarchy. Romanticism in this second sense is the claim of supreme authority made in behalf of a single feeling. The first is a tolerant, the second an intolerant romanticism.

With the first of these romanticisms the humanistic spirit is allied; or would be allied if it were not for the accidents of its origin. A tolerant romanticism is repugnant, not to humanism, but to classicism. But this is an outgrowth of two historic factors of the Renaissance, its alliance with the past, and its acceptance of the rationalistic bias of Greek thought. Whether there are or are not fixed and universal principles of truth, of beauty or of goodness, that can be apprehended by the eye of reason and applied to the changing content of human experience, is a philosophical problem. The affirmative answer is a philosophical doctrine. Classicism is an indoctrinated humanism, which is not a humanism at all, since it imprisons the spirit of man, or commits him in advance to what he should be free to choose or reject. The possibility that feeling has its own peculiar insight, or that truth is experimental and changing, are alternatives which should not be outlawed in advance. And the spirit of romanticism, with its sympathetic receptivity, and its sensitiveness to diverse nuances of felt value, is more congenial to the spirit of humanism than is the acceptance of tradition, or the affirmation of a set of immutable standards.

And it is classicism, not humanism, that is opposed to modernism. When I speak of modernism I mean precisely that which makes this word a disparaging epithet rather than the name of a period of time. I mean the cult of the new when it is still shocking—not Cézanne but Picasso, not Franck but Bartok, not Ibsen but Gertrude Stein. I mean change in its most revolting or exciting aspect, when it seems to have little to condemn or commend it but novelty. It is ironical indeed that humanism should find itself resistant to change. There is no better elixir or surer test of the free spirit than the relish for novelty. Why should a mind that seeks expansion and would be aware of all the possibilities, shut its eyes to that which is for the first time emerging into view? There is no reason except the prejudices of classicism—the habitual posture of retrospect or the fixed conviction that the future can be discounted in advance through the possession of a priori principles. A prejudice for the novel is as enslaving as a prejudice for the past. Nearsightedness and farsightedness are equally blind. The true humanist will not face merely toward the past and the distant and the eternal; he will face toward the future, the near and the temporal. He will face all ways. He will be aware of all parts of the circumference and all horizons up to that moving center where he stands.

In short, science, humanitarianism, democracy, romanticism and modernism are the natural allies of humanism, converted into enemies by humanism's disloyalty to itself.

IV

A just estimate of the place of the humanities in modern life depends on holding fast to their essential meaning. Any agency or relationship or situation or activity which has a humanizing, that is, a liberalizing effect: which broadens learning, stimulates imagination, kindles sympathy, inspires a sense of human dignity, and imprints that bearing and form of intercourse proper to a man, may be termed "a humanity." Travel, friendship, marriage, experience in affairs are, or may be, in this sense, humanities. They may be and often are inhumane. The difference depends on the level of the relationship, or upon what the participants contribute in the way of attitude, background and experience. Travel may confirm prejudice; friendship and marriage may be founded on utility; vocation may be narrowed to livelihood, and citizenship to a perfunctory discharge of civil duties; all the functions of man may degenerate into routine. In order that these experiences of later years may yield the values of humanism, society devises the instrumentalities of education, hoping to inoculate men with humanism in their early years. Those who have had the germ of humanism firmly implanted may then find in travel, friendship, marriage, vocation and citizenship, as well as in their leisure pastimes, occasions favorable to its growth.

That educational institution which is in America charged with this function, is the so-called liberal arts college; and the method employed is to teach "subjects," "studies," or "courses," grouped under departments which are supposed to coincide with the branches of human knowledge. There has lately developed a practice of grouping these departments in turn under "divisions," a popular classification being: physical science, biological science, social science—*and* "the humanities." Now this is a most extraordinary arrangement. In an institution which professes to exist for the purpose of inculcating it, liberal culture is only one-quarter of the whole; and a nondescript quarter, occupying the place of a sort of rearguard appointed to pick up the stragglers and misfits which find no place higher up in the procession!

> We may, if we like [says a recent writer], think of all knowledge as assuming the form of a triangle, of which one apex is occupied by the natural and physical sciences, another by the social sciences and the third by the humanities. The natural and physical sciences deal with man's environment, the most remote as well as the most immediate; the social sciences with man in his associations with other men; while the humanities concern themselves with the manifestations of his spiritual existence.[29]

A tripartite division of the curriculum is better than a fourfold division. But the size of the fraction does not remove the paradox that the curriculum of a liberal arts college should be, by definition, illiberal. Nor does it conceal the fact that such

---

[29] Waldo G. Leland, "Recent Trends in the Humanities," *Science*, N.S., LXXIX, 281.

"divisions" are shallow and artificial. The literature which is comprised in "the humanities" deals with man's physical and social environment; and the works of physical and social science are "manifestations of his spiritual existence."

This embracing of departments within divisions has one merit. It signifies the groping for a unity that shall counteract the pulverizing effect of specialized research and administrative decentralization. Some years ago it happened that the university of which I am a member needed money at the same time for its departments of chemistry, business administration and fine arts. It is reported that the astute divine who was in charge of the drive addressed a group of likely prospects in New York City and called attention to the silk stockings of the ladies present. In their dyes, he said, they are chemistry; as commodities, they are business administration; while in their attractiveness to the eye, they are fine arts. Today he might have added that in the Japanese origin of their silk, they are international relations. The Bishop's desire to integrate the activities of a university was commendable, and since the drive realized $10,000,000, his method was pragmatically justified. In the long run, however, and especially in the more limited case of the liberal arts college, I should prefer to find the unity at the other extremity—in singleness of mind and purpose.

All subjects are capable of being so presented and so studied as to promote freedom. What is the explanation of the indubitable fact that these possibilities are little realized? We fall too readily into the supposition that the original inhumanity lies in the student; that a college or university is a place where humane teachers are endeavoring to humanize unregenerate students. There is some truth, perhaps equal truth, in the view that a college is a place where students who are predisposed to humanity by the ardor and naïveté of youth endeavor more or less effectively to preserve their humanism under the influence of inhumane teachers. Institutions dedicated to humanism perpetually develop agencies which thwart this purpose. There are four such dehumanizing influences that may be singled out for special mention—technique, the multiplication of accessory disciplines, departmental separation, and vocational utility. Technique tends to become a game played for its own sake. It tends to divorce expertness from significance, and thus to trivialize research and blind both student and teacher to the purposes by which technique is justified. Owing to the extension of knowledge, the cult of thoroughness and precision, and the intellectual division of labor, "there is," to quote Professor Dodds, "a continual hiving off of specialists from the central swarm."[30] This multiplication of more or less autonomous entities is aggravated by the artificial barriers of academic departments, created for administrative purposes, but profoundly affecting the intellectual life of those who live *within* them. Finally, since the teacher has his job, and the student hopes to find one, it is inevitable that both should have an eye to the market for their wares. The teachers of the present era have been affected by all of these tendencies. All teachers were, during their most formative period, students. They are products of the system which is now entrusted to their keeping. They have been reared in laboratories, classrooms, and departments, where they have become habituated to some specialized procedure, and where they have looked upon their acquisitions as the tools of a trade. I do not say that these tendencies are either preventable or undesirable. But in some degree they militate against the teacher's realizing those humane possibilities which his subject, whatever it is, possesses.

Although any subject *may* be humanized or dehumanized, some subjects are more easily humanized or less easily dehumanized than others. Natural science is beset by all of the

---

[30] E. R. Dodds, *Humanism and Technique in Greek Studies,* Inaugural Lecture as Regius Professor, Oxford, 1936, p. 6.

dehumanizing influences that infest an educational institution. It is highly technical, and encourages the repetition of operations with no sense of their significance. In the interest of technical precision it has become highly abstract. Nature is stripped of its sensuous covering and its qualitative diversity. The natural sciences once put a premium upon sensibility—this was when the scientist visited and observed nature in its own habitat. Now he carries specimens of it into the laboratory. Even the astronomer has been displaced by the camera at the end of the telescope. Although the geologist still makes voyages of discovery upon the surface of the planet, he is being superseded by the geophysicist. The time seems to be approaching when the scientist will need no senses at all, except to read a needle or construct a graph, and these humble offices can be performed by a laboratory assistant. Nature is converted into symbols and concepts: it ceases to be natural.

Natural science is not only technical but technological. It provides instrumentalities of control, which are either determinately or indeterminately useful. In the former case they are subordinated to ulterior ends, such as war or material wealth, which are not of their own choosing. In the latter case they are divorced from ulterior ends altogether. Generalized utility may, like money, enrich its possessors with unappropriated resources, and so enlarge the range of possible attainment; but the scientist, like the money-maker, may become a miser or mere lover of power.

Natural science has other aspects which entitle it to be numbered among humanistic studies, but the proponents of science cannot, I think, be counted upon to do these justice. Professor George Sarton, in his *History of Science and the New Humanism,* emphasizes the passion for truth, the joy of its contemplation, and the testimony of science to the genius of man. He advocates the teaching of the history of science because this calls attention to its human origin. But like all proponents of natural science he stresses its utility, and thereby plays into the hands of his enemies. Indeed it would be difficult to find a better instance with which to sharpen the antithesis of science and humanity than that which he himself employs. Science, he says, has created the printing press and the radio, and has thus brought the "immortal plays" of Shakespeare, in both written and oral form, within the reach of "the poorest boy."[31] In other words, science is to the humanities as the radio to Shakespeare, or as the printing press to that which is worth printing. The first provides the means, the second the end from which the value of the means is derived. It is better to study Shakespeare than to study typesetting or communication engineering. The means is most economically obtained by purchase or hire; the end, the enjoyment of Shakespeare, is available only to those who experience it for themselves.

Natural science is unquestionably useful; indeed, it may be said to be the only thing that is useful. No claim for its utility can be too strong. Its utility lays mankind under an immense debt of gratitude. But the humanity of science does not lie in its utility, determinate or indeterminate. In saying this I do not disparage science, but protest against its own self-disparagement. I am contending that natural science is more than useful: it is also humane. Its humanity lies, on the one hand, in its revelation of the actual world as the environment and source of human life. If it is to fulfil this function of cosmic illumination it must be integrated and assimilated to personal experience, thus enabling men to choose the ends of action in the fullest possible view of *nature*. Its humanity lies in its illustration of the faculties of men—as a manifestation of reason, imagination, scrupulousness and disinterested-

---

[31] George Sarton, *The History of Science and the New Humanism*, 1937, pp. 13-14, 27-9, 124-5, 127. cf. also T. H. Huxley, "A Liberal Education," *op. cit.*, pp. 31-5; Leonard Huxley, *Life and Letters of Thomas Henry Huxley*, 1900, I, 219.

ness—in its non-acquisitive enjoyment of truth, and in its alliance with those cultural activities which unite men and contribute to their common heritage.

These humanistic functions of natural science do not take care of themselves. The inhumanity of natural science lies in the fact that it perpetually dehumanizes itself. Its strength arises from its technique, and its credit from its technology. But scientists may be both strong and famous without humanity. To preserve the humanity of science requires scientists who are so incorrigibly humane as to resist or transcend the influence of their own schooling and the popular applause of their usefulness.

It might be supposed that the social sciences, since they profess to deal with man, were inescapably humanistic. But humanism, alas! is always escapable. The social sciences were once identified with moral philosophy. Politics, economics, anthropology, sociology and jurisprudence were once concerned with the good life, or with the definition of the purposes for which institutions exist and by which they may be appraised. During the period of their recent efflorescence they have aspired to the technical method and the technological rôle of physical science. It would be fatuous to quarrel with this development. But in so far as the social sciences identify themselves with natural science, they must content themselves with the same limited humanistic values. They will be humane in so far, and only in so far, as they illuminate the actual world in which man lives, and testify to human capacity. Though they debase man in the content of their report, they may yet ennoble him as its author. Thus, for example, an anthropological colleague of mine has offered a lame apology for man, that "zoological upstart," before the accusing scrutiny of the anthropoid ape. This is the inverse of humanism, and degrades man rather than exalts him, until one recalls that Professor E. A. Hooton is himself a man, and illustrates, in a *jeu d'esprit* entitled *Apes, Men and Morons,*

A Definition of the Humanities 37

man's unique capacity to review his own history, and to be, if not edified, then at least amused.

The question of social goods and social ends still remains. It is not abolished through being excluded from a strictly scientific social science. Somewhere, at some time, somebody must consciously and thoughtfully adopt a purpose for the state, or for industry and commerce, for law, for life, and for organized society in general; and if the social sciences prefer to ignore this choice, then their distinctive claim to humanity is transferred to philosophy.

History faces a similar dilemma. It embraces fact-finding, and develops the accessory techniques. It reveals relations of cause and effect which it is useful to know. In exercising this function history shares the humanity of natural science. It exhibits the human genius of the historian. In particular, it unfolds the spectacle of time and extends the horizon of life. It is the right of the humanities, says Professor Jones, "to insist that the educated man should be free, not merely of his own time and clime, but of all times and cultures."[32] The knowledge of history, in short, frees men from the unconscious effects of history. It does not bestow this freedom unless it opens a wide prospect. A man is no freer when imprisoned in the thirteenth century than when imprisoned in his own. He is freed from both in proportion as he sees their relations and discounts their relativities.

But history is eminently humane in so far as it presents events under the aspect of human purposes and needs. History will have exercised a humanizing influence upon him who through its study has come to participate in the life of the race, to regard its quarrels as domestic quarrels, and to feel that he is in some sense commissioned to complete the unfulfilled task of his predecessors. History stands high

[32] Howard Mumford Jones, "The Relation of the Humanities to General Education," in *General Education*, edited by W. S. Gray, University of Chicago Press, 1934, p. 49.

among the humanities because it has not yet succeeded, despite the efforts of some of its friends, in becoming a social science, in the sense in which social science seeks to become a natural science. History still deals with history, that is, with deeds, with unique events, with individuals, groups and epochs bearing proper names, and with the goods and evils that beset the path of man in his attempts to achieve his ends. These humanizing encounters with life it is impossible for the historian, despite his statistics, his causes and effects, and his cycles, wholly to obscure. Owing to this relatively incurable humanity, history deserves to be classified as "a humanity" in the privileged sense.

The effect of the extension of the technique and technology of the physical sciences into the domain of the social sciences, and of philosophy and religion, is to exalt the rôle of "poetry." When the positivist wishes to express his contempt for the sensuous investiture of nature, or for feeling, intuition, or speculative thought, he allocates these to *mere* poetry. These rejections form so notable a part of human experience that they increase the dignity of poetry and threaten it, without any pretensions on its own part, with becoming the sole repository of the humanities. Let us broaden the conception of poetry to embrace the remainder of literature and the remainder of the arts. These are the studies which all agree to include within "the humanities," and to which some would award that title exclusively.

The humanities being, defined relatively to the curriculum, as those studies which inhumane teachers cannot completely dehumanize, literature and the arts possess an uncommonly stubborn humanity. Courses on literature, for example, are bound to present the literature, and this is humane. The literature will speak for itself in a voice that is never wholly drowned by the hum of academic machinery. Studies accessory to literature, such as phonetics, grammar, linguistics, comparative philology, semantics, are easily dehumanized—

A Definition of the Humanities

more easily, perhaps, than the physical or social sciences. Latin or Greek conceived as a "tool" for science, or as accessory to modern language, is, of course, not a humanity. The acquirement of the rudiments of a language is not in itself a humanizing experience. When language is a foreign language, especially when it is a dead foreign language, its mastery postpones and sometimes prohibits the humanistic result. "It is only a very strong man," says Huxley, "who can appreciate the charms of a landscape as he is toiling up a steep hill, along a bad road. The ordinary schoolboy . . . finds Parnassus uncommonly steep."[33] But in courses on Sophocles, Dante or Shakespeare, it is difficult wholly to counteract the effect of Sophocles, Dante and Shakespeare. A course on the documentary technique of attribution, or the chemical technique of restoration, or the historical sources of style, or the administration of museums, though given by a department of fine arts, is easily dehumanized; but he who offers instruction on Titian, Velasquez or Rembrandt must risk the chance that his students will see and enjoy Titian, Velasquez or Rembrandt.

The content of literature and of the arts is intrinsically humane. It presents life concretely, presenting models for admiration or condemnation—for imitation or rejection. It enlarges the range of immediate experience, and communicates it feelingly; it stimulates the imagination and breaks the moulds of habit; it expresses the diverse visions and aspirations of great men; it integrates the different cultural elements of a society or an epoch; it embodies beauty and commends it as an object of disinterested pleasure; at its best, it brings a sense of moral elevation.

Finally, philosophy. Here also it is possible, though not easy, to obscure the humanity that is inherent in the subject-matter. The history of philosophy, especially when associated

---

[33] "A Liberal Education," *op. cit.*, p. 45.

with the study of texts, breeds its pedants. It may through dwelling on psychological genesis reduce philosophical thinking to the natural science of psycho-pathology, or to the social science of historical causation. It may be used as an instrument of apologetics or propaganda. But it is difficult so to teach the history of philosophy as to avoid the multiplication and dissemination of intellectual alternatives. It is difficult to teach systematic philosophy without broadening horizons and encouraging the ordering of ideas. Metaphysics raises doubts and excites speculation: it will almost inevitably "joggle the mind," to use Emily Dickinson's expression.[34] "Philosophy," said William James, "is able to fancy everything different from what it is. It sees the familiar as if it were strange, and the strange as if it were familiar. It can take things up and lay them down again. Its mind is full of air that plays around every subject. It rouses us from our native dogmatic slumber and breaks up our caked prejudices."[35] For Bergson philosophy is essentially an act of freedom, since it proceeds, or will proceed when it *is* philosophy, to the completest possible integration of experience.

> Philosophy ... submits to criticism the ultimate principles of thought and action; it attaches no value to truth passively received; it would have each one of us reconquer truth by reflexion, earn it by effort; and, embracing it in the depths of our own self and animating it with our own life, lend it strength enough to fertilize thought and direct the will.[36]

The place of philosophy in a liberal arts college will depend upon the extent to which other subjects realize or renounce their humanistic possibilities. If the natural sciences confine themselves to technique and technology, then it will fall to

[34] Quoted by P. H. Boynton, *More Contemporary Americans*, 1927, p. 2.
[35] *Some Problems of Philosophy*, 1911, p. 7.
[36] Henri Bergson, address on "Le Bon-Sens et l'éducation," given in 1895, and quoted by A. Ruhe and N. M. Paul, *op. cit.*, p. 22.

philosophy to delineate the spectacle of nature in a course on "cosmology"; and to present the scientific spirit of man in a course on "the philosophy of science." If the social sciences yield their automony and become a province of natural science, then the meaning of society and the purposes of human institutions will be left to a course on ethics, theory of value or social philosophy. If history ceases to reconstruct and interpret the life of man, then that task will fall to a philosophy of history. If literature and the fine arts are superseded by their accessories and adjuncts, the history of philosophy, or aesthetics, or a philosophy of criticism will become the sole exponent of the intuitions and values of which literature and the fine arts are the vehicle.

In short, the extent to which a philosophical segment of the curriculum must carry the burden of humanism will depend on the extent to which other subjects or departments have abandoned their humanistic birthright.

In conclusion let me repeat that the justification of "the humanities" lies in their gift of freedom or enlightened choice. This gift is appropriate to every man by virtue of his generic nature. If men have any rights at all, they have a right to this, in the highest degree consistent with innate capacity. In a democracy, which in principle concedes equal opportunity to all, there can be no justice in denying this right to any man. If a man's inescapable limitations of capacity prevent his going beyond a certain level of attainment, then it is the business of society to carry something of freedom down to that level—to the secondary school, to the primary school, and to the kindergarten.

In an institution expressly devoted to liberal education, there should be no studies which do not in some measure contribute to the students' liberalizing experience. Every study is a potential humanity, even professional studies; so that there need be no complete estrangement between the liberal college and its attendant group of professional and technical schools.

All studies are humanities, when, as they may be, their humanistic possibilities are realized in intercourse between the seasoned humanity of the teacher and the innocent humanity of the student. But these auspicious conditions cannot be guaranteed. Hence the importance of giving prominence in a curriculum of liberal education to those studies which are so stubbornly humanistic that they can scarcely fail to distil some humanism even between uninspired teachers and unreceptive students. Hence the indispensable rôle of *"the* humanities," the humanities *par excellence,* such as history, literature, art and philosophy. These studies afford the highest probability in the long run that students, even if they do not want it, will obtain from teachers, even though these do not have it, some slight trace of that freedom, of that learning, imagination and sympathy, of that dignity and demeanor proper to a man, which I have here called "humanity."

HISTORY AND THE HUMANITIES
By August Charles Krey

HISTORY AND THE HUMANITIES

I

THE general purpose of these discussions, I understand, is to analyze the meaning of the humanities in relation to the various fields of learning; and my particular task is to consider this problem from the standpoint of the historian. This, I take it, is a twofold responsibility involving an examination, first, of the place of the humanities in history and, secondly, of the relationship existing between history and the humanities in the past and today.

As my own experience suggests, the problem of the humanities is no new one to the mediaeval historian, who has long been accustomed to regard the whole pattern of man's activities as his proper concern. How could he fail to do so? For in the Middle Ages politics was inextricably interwoven with religion; and with religion was associated the wide range of social, intellectual, eleemosynary, and artistic undertakings in which the organized church engaged. Likewise, the economic conditions of the period were of great concern to both church and state. The mediaevalist, therefore, came early to the conclusion that every activity of society during this period was of potential significance, and that, since the humanities interested mediaeval people, they also interest him.

The questions centering around the humanities are, however, of more than incidental concern to the historian of this period. As he moves on through its centuries, he finds his vision obscured, in the fourteenth century, by the formidable terms, Humanism and the Renaissance. He is asked, then, to recognize humanism as a new phenomenon and Petrarch as its creator. And, more than that, along with Petrarch and humanism, he is called upon to recognize the dawn of a new era named the Renaissance. These terms are not of the historian's own coining and the concepts which they describe, or veil, are not his either. He has been led to a reluctant acquiescence in their use only by the enthusiasm with which some of his friends have accepted them. I believe that he has never been quite happy in employing the words, which he always approaches gingerly and with some embarrassment. For his mind, like Edmund Burke's, is perpetually troubled by the effort to discover "what simple ideas, things, events and circumstances are included in these pulpy aggregates," called humanism and the Renaissance.

The main cycle of events which they represent is clear enough. With Petrarch, the historian is told, humanism begins. Thereafter humanists continue to appear in ever-increasing number. Boccaccio espouses the new learning. John of Ravenna teaches it to groups of disciples at Florence, Milan and Venice. Coluccio Salutati and Niccolo Niccoli promote it. Within fifty years after the death of its founder, the movement numbers such persons as Leonardo Bruni, Poggio, Filelfo, Guarino, Lorenzo Valla, Vittorino da Feltre—all major luminaries among a much greater number of followers, and humanism is but just started. Another half-century passes, and its devotees include the mighty of Italy. Two popes, practising humanists themselves, and many princes both of state and commerce are equipped with the new education. By this time, Italy is no longer large enough to hold the swelling numbers. They burst across the Alps to Germany, France, Spain, Hungary, and England. Reuchlin and Agricola, Budaeus and Lefevre, Ximenes, Vives, Grocyn and Linacre, not to forget Erasmus, challenge comparison with any of the distinguished humanists in Italy. Thereafter the movement widens and deepens, becoming a permanent part of the intellectual equipment of modern times.

The historian is distressed, not by the rather attractive name given to all this burgeoning of intellectual activity, but by the narrowness of its application. That is, he has much difficulty in discovering among the activities of the humanists anything which he has not met before.

Much stress is laid, for example, on the fact that the humanists were collectors of manuscripts and builders of libraries. That passion, however, had existed in the earlier centuries, when the library of York, for instance, was celebrated in verse, and when Fulda, St. Gall and other monasteries likewise gained great renown for their collections. Was not Gerbert himself accused of plundering the library of Bobbio, perhaps to enrich that of Rheims? Rulers, too, are known to have accumulated libraries, even though they housed them in church buildings. Did not Vincent of Beauvais dip freely into the capacious purse of St. Louis to build up a royal library in Paris? Indeed, it is rather surprising to note how many of the major discoveries of classical manuscripts so enthusiastically applauded by the humanists of Italy were made in libraries north of the Alps.

Or, again, much is made of the intensive study which the humanists gave to the ancients, and of their success in eliminating corruptions introduced by copyists. But the classics had been studied all during the Middle Ages, when Greek was not altogether unknown, and when grammars had been written at intervals. Even books of style were not unknown; and John of Garland is certainly reckoned a distinguished scholar in this branch of what was later to be called philology, though more than a century was to pass before Petrarch began to achieve his reputation and two before Valla was to establish a new norm in such matters. As for the errors of copyists in the corruption of texts, did not Alcuin, as early as the late eighth century, persuade the mighty Charlemagne to issue a capitulary on this subject? And did any of the Renaissance humanists urge more truculently than Roger Bacon the need for establishing correct texts by a nice study of language and by a careful collation of manuscript copies? Certainly the classical learning and interest in libraries cannot be said to have begun with the Renaissance.

More emphasis, of course, is placed on the aesthetic appreciation of the classics by the humanists, on their interest in the style of the ancient authors, on their discriminating taste and their modelling of their own writings on the best work of the past. Yet, even in these respects the historian is troubled. Certainly, Bede was not innocent of style, as is displayed both in his own volumes and in his choice of reading material. The scholars who learned from Alcuin and vied with each other in composing both poetry and prose on classical models were more than dimly aware of what Horace calls the "glory and charm" of words. Virgil and Terence, Cicero and Seneca, Livy and Sallust are all clearly recognized as superior stylists not only by Lupus Servatus, Theodulphus, Angilbert, and Eginhard, but also by later writers of the Middle Ages. Does not the nun of Gandersheim compel Terence to pious uses? And, according to Lambert of Hersfeld, does not Henry IV make his memorable journey over the Alps to Canossa in the words of Livy?

Furthermore, long before the fourteenth century, appreciation of good writing was rather widespread. For example, all France seemed to shudder at the barbarous style used by the anonymous writer of the Gesta in presenting the story of the First Crusade. Thereupon at least three writers, all men of position, one of them Guibert de Nogent, undertook, with more ambition than success, to rewrite the chronicle. And this happened two centuries and a half before Petrarch proclaimed the new era. Ekkehard of Aura and Otto of Freising may be a bit difficult to read, but no one can deny their conscious use of classical models. John of Salisbury, William of Tyre, and, after them, the historians of Henry II's reign, particularly Matthew of Paris, can scarcely be impugned either for their own performance or for their choice of models. Many of the humanists of the Renaissance wrote far worse Latin than did these authors. Nor did the writers of the pre-Renaissance times regard their efforts at style altogether as penitential labors calculated to insure their speedier salvation. John of Salisbury's reiterated repetition of Quintillian's observation that "otium sine litteris mors est vivique hominis sepultura" suggests a resigned willingness to postpone that state in favor of a longer lingering among the classical writers. There is no reason to suppose that he was alone, among the writers before the Renaissance, in harboring such emotions. Nor need we join Symonds in exploring the poetic outbursts of ebullient undergraduates to understand that there was joy in letters during the centuries before Petrarch and Boccaccio. There were many past forty who felt that delight—the same delight which (as Catullus complained) still excites a reader to sleeplessness when he comes upon an unusually fine passage of prose or poetry.

Among some modern writers on humanism there is also evidence of a tendency to identify that movement with knowledge of Greek. That, however, is a distinction which it would be difficult to maintain and one which neither the majority, nor the most thoughtful, of commentators would care to accept. Indeed, this measure of discrimination would eliminate many who have an enduring claim upon this title. It would, among others, eliminate Petrarch himself. Equally embarrassing, on such a basis, would be the compulsion to extend the ranks of humanists, for Greek was not altogether unknown in the earlier centuries. John Scotus certainly knew that language, as did also scattered scholars in the centuries that followed. During the twelfth and thirteenth centuries there appear to have been scholars capable of extensive and even accurate translations from the Greek. Both John of Salisbury and Roger Bacon knew as much, if not more, Greek than Petrarch did.

Even the conflict between the devotees of the classics and the dialecticians, about which so much is said in the period of the Renaissance, is not unknown in the earlier centuries. John of Salisbury, for example, balances the variant arguments bearing on the education of a scholar, while Roger Bacon denies the efficacy of dialectics as a sound approach even to a theological career. Both denounce the hair-splitting of the dialecticians; and John, at least, emphasizes the greater and more lasting satisfaction to be found in the study of the classics. Nor does the contrast between secular and clerical scholarship establish any effective demarcation between the age of Petrarch and the earlier time. That distinction falls down on both sides, for not only were many of the recognized humanists churchmen, but there were secular scholars in the previous period also.

In the face of all this knowledge it has been indeed very difficult for the historian to be comfortable in the thought that with Petrarch a new age dawns. To be sure Petrarch rather intimated that such was his own opinion of his importance. But so did Leonardo Bruni, more than a generation after Petrarch. Neither, however, was by profession an historian and each had something to sell. Doubtless the so-called novelty of their wares enhanced their value in the eyes of some. Such an advertisement is a common selling device; and even historians have been known to use it, as one member of the profession had occasion to imply recently in a paper on the eighteenth century "when," he observed, "the 'new history' was somewhat newer than it is today." Thus, surveying all that counts, the historian is forced to deny the novelty of that humanistic flowering in the fourteenth century commonly called the Renaissance.

To be sure, he has usually refrained from direct denial, and has sought, instead, to reconcile his historical conscience by expanding the terms to cover some of the more prominent earlier occurrences of the phenomena. Thus, Munro and Haskins both refer to the "Renaissance of the twelfth century"; and others, like C. W. C. Davis, have applied the term to the period of Charlemagne, naming it the Carolingian Renaissance. In time, doubtless, someone will thus describe the period of the Saxon Emperors in Germany and the age of Alfred in England. Then we may have also the Ottonian or the Alfredian Renaissance.

This wider usage of the terms indicates the reluctance of the historian to admit that there is any distinctive difference, at least in quality and on major counts, between the activities of the so-called humanists of the fourteenth, fifteenth, and sixteenth centuries and the work of scholars before that time. That is, the movement must be studied in perspective and in process of development when at times it lay almost dormant, only slowly rising to the effulgence of the Renaissance. During this long time, such variations as can be detected are rather of quantity than quality. There is, at one time and another, a difference in the amount of work done in each of the activities, a difference in the number of persons engaged. These dissimilarities also appear in the other periods to which the name Renaissance has been applied as well as in those to which it might be applied. The development, however, is, in any case, not one of steady progression. Some of these renaissances, though coming later, include fewer humanists and accomplish less, while others, occurring earlier, are marked by more brilliance. In short, the Renaissance which opens in the fourteenth century is set apart from the others not intrinsically, but only measureably. That is, at this time there are more scholars producing more, but not necessarily better, work than in the preceding centuries.

II

And yet, having said all this, the student of this period can not be entirely satisfied that he has done more than describe certain circumstances. He has offered no explanation either of their occurrence or their efflorescence. True he has placed and named the leading humanists—has analyzed and described their activities. But how was it that these activities, which were a source of pleasure to them, were also vocations yielding a product which could be exchanged for material benefits willingly contributed by other members of society? If the historian has found nothing sufficiently distinctive in the activities of the humanists to justify the recognition of a new era, will he find it in the environment surrounding, encouraging, and supporting them?

Following this cue, Petrarch's career might be examined in terms of his education, his associates, his tendencies, his opportunities, and in terms also of the pressures which operated upon him. It is not my purpose, however, to trace in detail a career already familiar to you all, but merely to emphasize certain aspects of it which call attention to the soil out of which his genius grew.

Florentine, born in exile, son of a notary whose means were insufficient to maintain him in idleness, the lad was moved about from place to place as his father's opportunities for employment dictated. The father finally found a haven at Avignon, then the seat of the papal court, and lived barely long enough to provide for his son's education. The boy gave early evidence of enough mental ability to justify the hope that he, too, might become a notary, or even a full-fledged lawyer.

The family income was sufficient to maintain him in comfort during his school days, but no longer, as is evidenced by the fact that, on the death of his father, the young man had to leave Bologna before completing his course. He was therefore constantly aware of the relationship of his college education to a gainful career. Though recognizing this fact by a satisfactory attention to his school subjects, he did not allow it to restrain the normal exuberance of youth. He attended carefully to his dress, and like many another young man, composed amatory lyrics which found great favor with his classmates, if not also with the objects of his fancy. He seems also to have won friends through his scholastic abilities, the rich stores of his knowledge doubtless serving his associates well upon critical occasions. These college friendships were to prove very advantageous to him later.

Thus far, his career was only that of hundreds who before him had shown similar tastes and similar abilities. Had he lived in another age, he might probably have developed into a Lupus Servatus, a Guibert de Nogent, or any one of many. Living when he did, the end was to be different. Thanks to his college friendships, he was soon drawn into the circle of the Colonna at Avignon. These members of the proud Roman family were none too happy on that French soil, away from the administration of their own estates and their customary feuds with the Orsini and other feudal politicians. It was for them a period of exile with its usual accompanying nostalgia. Under such circumstances, everything connected with Rome became doubly dear. None suffered from homesickness more than the head of the group, the Cardinal Giovanni, whose interest in theology was but slight and in larger ecclesiastical politics only moderate. He, therefore, comforted himself by gathering together a variety of material regarding ancient Rome, its archaeological remains and its literature. With this man young Petrarch found employment as a secretary. The sentimental interests of the Cardinal immediately provoked a very congenial response in his assistant, whose business at Court necessitated the use of Latin and whose attention was drawn, by the hobby of his employer, toward classical literature. Doubtless, too, the Cardinal lost no opportunity of advancing his protégé's interests.

The kind of writing which Petrarch did as secretary, whether on more sober business or in those playful letters on classical authors which must have delighted the Cardinal, soon attracted enough attention to turn the head of any young man. The circle of his correspondents grew on both sides of the Alps, and the demand for his letters increased. Nor was this demand lessened after Petrarch had himself crowned poet laureate in Rome. This was a whim of vanity which the old Cardinal may well have indulged him, and the reception of the young man by King Robert of Naples was no doubt made possible through the same influences.

Literary skill and fortunate friendships thus secured for Petrarch many favors. At first these were at the papal court and in the form of ecclesiastical benefices, the customary support for writers of Latin. But the secular demand for, and appreciation of, his writings was soon so great that, assured of a satisfactory living at princely courts, he was able to abandon the church benefices.

The point of departure in Petrarch's career arrives when he leaves Avignon. Had he continued to depend on his churchly connections, he might have become increasingly immersed in ecclesiastical affairs and have ended his days as an abbot or a bishop. Instead he found a secular world not only ready but eager to receive him, ready to indulge him in the continued pursuit of his intellectual inclinations and to maintain him in even more comfortable circumstances than he had thus far enjoyed.

The willingness of princely courts such as those of the Visconti at Milan to entertain a literary figure is, of course, no strikingly new phenomenon. Rulers and courts of other days had been equally hospitable to men of letters. Charlemagne, Otto, Alfred, the Capetians, Philip II, Louis IX and Philip IV, the Normans and Angevins, William the Conqueror, Henry I, Henry II and Edward I and, in Italy, Roger of Sicily and Frederick II—all these are listed among the most prominent instances of such earlier secular patronage. The difference, again, lies not in the quality of such patronage but in its relative quantity. There was now not merely one such court in Italy but several; and Petrarch was able to move from one to another without serious difficulty.

The most significant difference in the times, however, is that suggested by Petrarch's account of his visit to the goldsmith of Bergamo. This man, distinguished in his craft, had accumulated a comfortable fortune by middle age and had then retired from active work to devote himself to the study of Latin literature. Petrarch marvelled at the evidences of taste revealed in the goldsmith's home, not merely in its appointments, but also in its library which included, besides classical authors, as many of the poet's own writings as his host had been able to purchase. I cite this instance not only because Petrarch has described this individual at some length, but because one wonders if there were not many other citizens like him among the numerous anonymous admirers to whom Petrarch alludes. Such an hypothesis receives additional support in the generous and flattering invitations he received from the two mercantile cities, Florence and Venice. Indeed, the whole career of this young artist seems to suggest the emergence at this time of an enlarged leisured class interested in letters.

Possibly earlier instances could be found of such concern among the burghers. Historians of the twelfth century might point to the *fabliaux,* for example, as indicative of such literary interest. Later in the century or early in the next, the satirical literature represented by Meier Helmbrecht surely reflects the same turning of attention—an attention which, increased in volume and more serious in nature, welcomed in the thirteenth century the appearance of histories in the vernacular. Perhaps, too, it is that interest which accounts for those imposing didactic poems, the *Romance of the Rose* and the *Divine Comedy* as well as the encyclopedic *Tresor* of Brunetto Latini. Such works might well have appealed to men whose wits were keen enough to procure for them a period of leisure, even if relatively late in life. It would be difficult indeed to account for the popularity of books of this kind solely on the basis of demand by a class still chiefly devoted to horses, tournaments, battles, and romance.

If these conjectures are true, they would appear to indicate a rapidly growing participation in letters by a new group with time to spare—a group which was gaining not only in numbers but in seriousness of interest as well. If this group was content, in the twelfth century, to be satisfied with satirical jibes at the privileged orders, and had advanced, in the next century, to share in the learning of the schools, diluted as that had to be in the vernacular, it might well have become ready, in the following century, to study Latin in order more fully to tap the stores of learning. The uncertainties which Dante voices about the use of Latin or the vernacular in his *De Vulgari Eloquentia* indicates the threshold of exactly such development. A generation after him, that threshold is fully crossed, and the lay world is ready for the kind of learning and writing which Petrarch promotes. If this conjecture is valid, it would seem, then, that Boccaccio, in shifting from the vernacular to the Latin, was not so much changing his audience as meeting its new and enlarged demands.

Behind the development of humanism, as exemplified in Petrarch's career, there was, then, apparently an advance in the intellectual demands of the new leisure class.

III

This theory may be tested by a more extensive examination of the small non-professional group with whom humanism begins in Florence. Boccaccio died in 1375; but before his death, Colluccio Salutati, a notary, had begun to cultivate the new interest in classical letters. Though he continued in the practice of his profession, he managed to combine with it his avocational hobby, thus setting a new style in his papers as Chancellor of Florence. His understudy, Leonardo Bruni, learned both vocation and avocation from him, with emphasis upon the latter. The two other leaders in the development of humanism, Palla Strozzi and Niccolo Niccoli, were businessmen, the first a banker and the other trained as a merchant. These were the men who promoted the humanistic studies in Florence and made that city the leader in this field for nearly a century.

Niccolo Niccoli's activities, in particular, will justify somewhat thorough study. One of four sons of a very prosperous Florentine merchant, trained like his brothers for a practical mercantile career, he decided not long after his father's death to leave the care of the business to his three brothers. Presumably he derived an income from his share of his father's estate and was therefore free to devote himself enthusiastically to the new learning, filling his bachelor apartments with pieces of ancient sculpture, jewelry, and other archaeological treasures. His chief energy, however, was spent in collecting ancient manuscripts—Greek as well as Latin. Through numerous correspondents over the whole Florentine commercial network, he sought out manuscripts, purchasing them or paying for their transcription, and by the time of his death he had accumulated a total of eight hundred. At that time, however, his enthusiasm—like that of most booklovers—had quite outrun his resources, so that he left behind him a considerable debt as well as a large library.

His career is somewhat puzzling in that he appears to have been one of the few prominent Florentines not engaged in a gainful occupation. He is found frequently in the group which was wont to gather around the learned friar Ambrogio Traversari, to indulge in intellectual discussion. His bachelor quarters were a constant rendezvous for young and old who were interested in learning. It was his practice to provide each of his guests, as they entered, with some book fitted to their tastes, and at times as many as a dozen friends were to be found reading in his apartment. He was equally generous in lending his books, the executors of his estate finding some two hundred of them thus loaned at the time of his death.

He seems indeed to have been on terms of easy friendship with most of the important persons in Florence. Though he lived through the transition from the oligarchical domination of Florence to that of Cosimo de Medici, he had warm friends on both sides of that controversy. With Palla Strozzi, he went about among the prominent Florentines to gather the funds with which to bring the learned Chrysolaras from Constantinople, to teach Greek in Florence in 1396. He was no less persuasive in procuring the support of Cosimo for similar encouragement of learning after 1434.

He interested himself especially in the young men, giving all who displayed exceptional ability ready access to his books, and using his influence in behalf of those who needed employment. Some of his protégés either became secretaries at the papal court or served wealthy patrons outside and inside Florence, Poggio Bracciolini and Carlo Aretino being among them. And, as is related by Vespasiano, he was even able to induce favored young Florentines to engage in study. Meeting young Piero Pazzi on the street one day, Niccolo asked him what he was doing, to which the latter replied airily, "Just giving myself a good time." Thereupon Niccolo rebuked him and urged him to better ways, saying, "As you are the son of such a father, and of such good presence, it is a shame that you should not take to the study of Latin which would make a polished man of you. If you neglect learning, you will win little esteem and when the flower of your youth has passed you will find yourself a good for nothing." The young man returned to him some days later and asked Niccolo to find him a proper instructor. The teacher whom Niccolo suggested taught not only young Pazzi, but also Piero de Medici, Cosimo's son, as well as the sons of several other wealthy Florentines.

In Niccolo's career, it seems to me, we have exemplified the dynamics of the humanistic development. He himself, like the goldsmith of Bergamo, took to the new learning as an adult, though apparently somewhat earlier than the latter. Perhaps he regretted that his father had not provided him with such an education in his youth. From his conversation with young Pazzi one judges that wealth had become sufficiently secure to permit anticipation of leisure and to justify education toward its enjoyment. The advantages of the new learning which Niccolo held out to Piero were, not a steady and remunerative job, but "polish" and "a worthwhile old age"—values which a number of prominent educators have recently asserted, are too little emphasized in American colleges. For Niccolo, as for the goldsmith of Bergamo, these ends, however, were doubtless chief, and sufficient, inducements.

The career of Palla Strozzi is likewise interesting—Strozzi, one of the oligarchy whom the Medici were to displace, and whose learning made him an especially effective ambassador for Florence on many occasions. When at the age of sixty-two he found himself an exile, he whiled away many weary hours by studying classical letters. Thus he passed more than twenty years in a foreign land not, like Odysseus, "ever sighing and weeping for his own dear land," but enjoying his books and his new friends. The interest he felt in learning evidently became a family heritage, for cultivated Strozzi continued to appear for many generations in northern Italy.

This compensatory value of the classics is even more vividly emphasized in the letter of Machiavelli, similarly exiled on a humble rural estate, to his friend Vettori—a letter which Cicero himself might have written from his Tusculan villa.

> . . . But when evening comes I return home and shut myself up in my study. Before I make my appearance in it, I take off my rustic garb soiled with mud and dirt and put on a dress adapted for courts and cities. Thus fitly habited I enter the antique resorts of the ancients; where being kindly received, I feed on that food which alone is mine and for

which I was born. For an interval of four hours I feel no annoyance, I forget every grief, I neither fear poverty nor death, but am totally immersed.

The group we are considering, however, relied on classical learning for more than comfort and amusement. They recognized that the "polish" to be derived from the study of Latin and Greek classics was apt to prove advantageous in many fields. They were clever enough to observe that Petrarch's conversation and writing, together with his ability to cloak the acts and persons of contemporary men in classical simile and metaphor, insured his welcome at any court or circle. Likewise, they recognized an even more practical side to this polish, as is revealed in the oft-repeated comment of Gian Galeazzo Visconti that a letter of Coluccio Salutati's, then Chancellor of Florence, was worth a thousand soldiers. Secretaries trained in the new learning soon became the fashion, the demand long continuing far in excess of the supply. Even the swashbuckler condottieri found a definite value in having their abilities and achievements described by such writers, who, in the fifteenth century, were supported at most of the little courts of the Romagna. We can still share the chagrin of the Florentines when their ill-trained gonfalonier failed to reply in kind to the eloquent Latin address of the Neapolitan ambassador, a chagrin all the deeper because there were present cultivated Florentines able and willing to make a proper reply. Florence, however, was seldom caught in such a plight and regularly sent on important embassies citizens who possessed humanistic learning. Such men she found of advantage even at the court of France, not then noted for its encouragement of letters. Indeed, by the end of the fifteenth century, the diplomatic value of men of cultivation had become so generally appreciated that not only did nearly all Italian courts, small as well as great, employ them, but so, too, did the important courts outside of Italy, notably Spain, France, and England.

It is a serious mistake, however, and one which is too commonly made, to think that "polish," personal distinction and a happier old age were the only values which the new leisure class sought or found in the study of the classics. They were interested in the substance as well as the form of that literature. They were keenly on the alert for any advice which the ancients might supply toward the solution of their own problems. This, I believe, was true of the humanistic movement in Italy from its beginnings in the fourteenth century throughout the period of the Renaissance.

One of the first lessons which they derived from such study was in the realm of education. Cicero's *Orator*, Plutarch's essay on education, and above all Quintillian's *Institutes*, now available in complete form, provided them with the blueprint for a new system of education. If we choose, we can trace this development all the way back to Petrarch, whose copyists were really apprentices in the new learning. The progress is more clearly defined in the career of Niccolo whose energetic efforts included the encouragement, not only of young scholars, but also of wealthy young men for whom, as for Piero, he procured teachers. His efforts were so successful that private tutors soon began to be superseded by distinguished teachers who received a number of promising pupils at their own homes.

Both as a result of the increased demand for such instruction and the more careful study of Quintillian, we reach the stage represented in the schools of Vittorino da Feltre at Mantua and of Guarino at Ferrara. These schools became institutions capable of indefinite perpetuation. Their fame attracted students and observers from a distance and they became models for similar establishments elsewhere. To them we owe, with remarkably little change in curriculum and even less in spirit, the lycée of France, the gymnasia of Germany, and the great public schools of England, not to overlook the best of our private preparatory schools in this country. The debt of all these schools to Quintillian is obvious, but in their emphasis upon the combination of mental, physical, and moral training, there is a definite accent derived from the needs of the fifteenth century. That this development was not a mere imitation of classical models is abundantly testified by the numerous treatises on education which continued to appear throughout that century and later.

These devotees of humanism also sought and found in classical writings much that ministered to the art of living, especially to human relationships. These lessons they applied all the way from the conduct of the family to the conduct of a court, indeed of a whole society. Here, as in the case of education, this dependence was not mere slavish imitation. Their findings were, in fact, based less upon a single classical work than upon a discriminating use of many bearing directly on their own needs. Thus, the *De re uxoria* of Francesco Barbaro, along with the works of Cicero and Plutarch, was esteemed a worthy guide for the management of a household. It is significant that a large share of the writings in this area of interest were not only in the vernacular, but composed at a time when, it is commonly thought, the language of the people was completely submerged. Among them may be cited Palmieri's *Della vita civile* and Alberti's *Libri della famiglia*. The application of classical learning to contemporary problems of human relationships is attested by the fact that the two greatest productions of Italian humanists were both written in the vernacular. I am referring, of course, to Castiglione's *Il Cortegiano* and Machiavelli's *Il Principe*. If the Greek and Latin classics, if Plato and Aristotle, Cicero, Seneca, Quintillian, and many others, can be recognized as classical sources, so too can the conditions of life in fifteenth and early sixteenth century Italy and Europe. In fact, for those interested in the effects of humanistic study upon the ideals of human intercourse, there is no more revealing exercise than to compare the court of Urbino with that of King Arthur, or Castiglione with Mallory.

The use of classical sources to throw light on contemporary problems is even more concretely revealed in the arts. Both literary and archaeological sources were drawn upon. Alberti, perhaps, reveals most fully the conscious process by which the fine arts of the Italian Renaissance—architecture, sculpture, and even painting—were influenced by the artist's knowledge of classical studies. Very few of these products, however, can be correctly described as pure imitation. Whether our taste entirely approves of all of them or not, we must recognize in them the use of past learning in the service of contemporary artistic problems.

No less practical was the use of classical learning in connection with the art of war. The interest of the Condottieri in the classics was by no means exhausted in hearing themselves compared to Caesar and Alexander, to the disparagement of the latter. They were also keen to study the tactics and strategy of the ancient generals, and they did not overlook the contributions which the ancients might make to the science of fortification and siege craft. Nor were literary scholars entirely innocent of calling to the attention of the Condottieri the help which artists might supply in the conduct of military activities.

This joining of talents is most highly dramatized by Caesar Borgia in whose campaigning both Machiavelli and Leonardo da Vinci shared, but it had also occurred much earlier in the fifteenth century and was to continue later. Though the armies of France and Spain had little to learn from the Italians about the wholesale destruction of the enemy, their generals had much to learn from them about the art of war, tactics and strategy, fortification and siege craft. Vitruvius and Vegetius, as well as the classical historians, both Greek and Latin, contributed to this knowledge, but so, also, did the experience of fifteenth century Italy.

If, however, one undertook to select a single individual to illustrate the relation of the new learning to practical affairs, it would be difficult to find a better example than Cosimo de Medici. Leading banker of Europe and for thirty years master of Florence—or "Pater Patriae" as the devoted citizens styled him—none was more deeply involved in the affairs of this world. Yet, he found time not merely to patronize scholars and artists, but to cultivate their society and, somehow or other, to do a great amount of reading as well. Apparently no subject was strange to him: he could discuss agriculture with farmers, and actually did prune his own vines; he could talk literature with men of letters, and theology with scholarly priests and monks; he was more than an amateur in law, and delighted in ethics and philosophy. His conversations with Pagolo on astrology are alluded to elsewhere. Architecture, sculpture, and painting, music and landscape gardening were more than passing fancies with him. His judgment and taste as displayed in his choice of certain artists to do particular pieces of work, as well as his dealings in finance and foreign affairs, have brought him deserved fame. Indeed, nearly all that he did in promoting scholarship, in building churches, in developing libraries, and in planning and equipping his own town and country homes, reflects a judicious blending of learning with a practical understanding of immediate conditions and requirements. However fantastic the Platonic Academy which he really founded may seem to us now, even that project was not without some bearing on trade with Greece and the Levant. And yet the genuine interest in Plato which he displayed at the very end of his life can scarcely fail to arouse the admiration of philosophers today. Few men in any age have combined wide learning with a knowledge of practical affairs to better advantage than did Cosimo.

Were further proof needed that the humanists did not esteem the classics for their style alone, it might be found in abundance in the content of the libraries being assembled at their instigation. That of the Duke of Urbino, which Vespasiano has described in some detail, may be regarded as a model. It contained what was then regarded as a complete library of works in Latin, Greek, and Hebrew. Scripture, the church fathers, and the mediaeval doctors of theology were all represented. So also were writings on civil law, including recent commentaries. All the chief writers on arithmetic, geometry, astrology, architecture, and military affairs were included as well as books on painting, sculpture, and music. The medical section contained mediaeval Arabic treatises in addition to Hippocrates and Galen. Furthermore, the library was enlarged by the works of "modern" Italian writers, both in Latin and in the vernacular, though of Boccaccio's writings only the Latin were included. The Italian were doubtless added by a less pious successor or book dealer. There were other libraries larger than this, but, according to Vespasiano, none more complete. Apparently, as is indicated in Niccolo's will, the practice of making books available to scholars and students was becoming widespread. Even so small a town as Pistoia could boast of a public library of one hundred and fifty volumes housed in the palace of the Signory.

IV

The examples which I have thus far cited have revealed, I hope, that the interest in classical literature was widespread among a developing merchant group and not confined either to aesthetes or erudite scholars. The instances are, however, drawn chiefly from those who might be called the patrons of humanism: that is, men of affairs to whom humanism was of incidental concern. Let us now consider those who made learning a profession.

The greater number of these, naturally, were teachers, either tutors in the homes of the wealthy or in schools like those at Ferrara or Mantua or in universities. Others were to be found at courts, where as secretaries they performed a variety of duties both useful and ornamental. It has been customary to regard these professional humanists as chiefly intent upon the restoration of antiquity, "Die wiederbelebung des Klassischen Altherthums," as Voigt puts it. Their ideal is reputed to have been to write Latin as Cicero wrote it; to describe the activities of life as the ancients might have done; to converse in the idiom of the Augustan age; even to discuss the mysteries of religion in terms of classical paganism. To this group of scholars is rather generally ascribed the substitution of a stilted, affected, artificial Latin style, ill adapted to the needs of contemporary life, in place of the natural, living, if less elegant, mediaeval Latin so adaptable to the ordinary demands of society.

If, however, we examine closely the careers of the professional humanists from Petrarch to Bembo and Erasmus, we shall be forced to admit that no one of them conforms exactly to such a pattern. True, we recognize in most of them a very definite regard for style and a common practice of embellishing their writings with quotations from ancient authors—a practice which Montaigne was later to condemn, not only as "filching-theft" but as "prejudicial to any trivial composer." Still, nearly all of the professional humanists were definitely concerned about the substance of their writings, and a singularly large proportion of them were interested not only in religion and the Church, but also in reading the Scriptures and the early church fathers out of the original Greek and Latin. Though they read and taught the pagan classics, they also wrote on early Christian theology. Such men are found throughout the period. There is a trace of this catholic interest in Petrarch and much more than a trace of it in Erasmus. It is pronounced in the careers of Luigi Marsigli and Fra

Ambrogio, in those of Ficino and Pico della Mirandola, as also in those of Lefevre, John Colet and Melancthon, not to mention many others who were high dignitaries of the Church.

It was perhaps only natural that many of the professional humanists were interested in law. Much of the early impulse toward humanism came from the legal profession; and much of the support of the movement continued to come from that source. A man trained only in the technicalities of the law might seem quite illiterate to the humanists, if not also to a wider society; but many lawyers, if not most, found some time for the cultivation of letters. Between the latter and the professional humanists there was a real and abiding affinity. Not only did some of the lawyers become so deeply imbued with classical lore that they could and did teach the classics, but some of the humanists made important contributions to law. It is unnecessary to recall the fact that Petrarch himself was trained as a lawyer, or that Colluccio Salutati, who remained a lawyer throughout his life, also taught the classics. Such examples are rather common throughout this period. Politian, usually regarded as the gay literary companion of Lorenzo the Magnificent, was also editor of the *Pandects of the Corpus Juris Civilis*. The combination of humanism and law continues to recur not only in Italy, but also in the more northern countries, as, witness, John Reuchlin in Germany and John Tiptoft and Thomas More in England. Indeed, one of the charges against the Earl of Worcester was that he had introduced some new laws which he had learned at Padua.

A surprisingly large number of professional humanists were also interested in subjects now generally termed science and technology. These found their outlet in translating from the Greek and in editing Latin works on natural history, cosmography, mathematics, and engineering of various kinds. Medicine, too, was included in their field of interest, not only as a subject of discussion and translation, but even of practice. Thus, Pagolo, friend of Cosimo de Medici, professor of astrology and other forms of mathematics, practised medicine for a few friends; thus, also, the uncle of Savonarola at Ferrara; or, a better example yet, the professor of philosophy, Fracostoro, who also practised medicine and wrote his famous description of the *Galli morbus* in verse.

It is apparently the fate of every intellectual advance to suffer a trailing band of semi-moronic followers who glory in belonging to a movement, but are less than vaguely aware of its real purpose. Just as the achievements of modern scientists tend to lose luster under a cloud of factual tabulators, so the real contributions of scholastic philosophers have been obscured by the logic-choppers who followed in their wake. Similarly, the humanists were cursed with a following incapable of doing more than imitating the classics. If, instead of staring at this sophomoric fringe, we follow the professors of humanism into their studies, we shall find almost none of them whose interest is confined to form alone. Even the schoolmaster, Guarino, found satisfaction in translating Strabo's work on geography.

To appreciate fully the intellectual activity stimulated by the development of humanism, we must, however, turn to the universities established in connection with the movement. Omitting the many incipient universities whose careers were more or less brief, we may confine our attention to four: Padua, Pavia, Pisa, and Ferrara.

Two of these may trace their actual origin to an earlier time, but all four owed their vitality to the force of humanistic studies, and should, therefore, be regarded as humanistic foundations. All of them were essentially city universities, that is, universities serving the intellectual demands of the city states: Padua serving Venice; Pavia, Milan; Pisa, Florence; and, finally, Ferrara, really an offshoot of Padua, owing its being to the influence of Guarino at the court of the Este family. All these universities were in close touch with their respective city patrons. Not only were they under the auspices of these cities, but there was a great deal of intermingling, and of constant visiting back and forth between faculty, students, and citizens. In the case of Florence, the university was actually divided, the humanities being kept at Florence for some time, while law, medicine, and theology were taught at Pisa. This did not mean that those at Pisa were without interest in the humanities. Benvenuto Cellini, for instance, on unveiling his Perseus at Florence, received many laudatory sonnets from the professors and students at Pisa, then on vacation. The University of Ferrara was, of course, located in that city, where there was, as elsewhere, a close intimacy between the leaders of the civic society and the university, the professors, and at times the students too, being invited to participate in the social life. Where there were courts, as at Milan and Ferrara and even at Florence under the Medici, leading scholars of all kinds were frequently found rubbing elbows with courtiers of varying interest in learning, humanistic or otherwise.

This intermingling of intellectual and lay interests both at universities and courts was to be extremely fruitful in the later development of learning. In such association the humanistic scholars learned to appreciate the justice of the high regard which the ancients extended to artists. These joint efforts proved valuable, whether they were enlisted, as at Venice in improving the design of ships and the science of navigation; or, as at Florence, in the planning and construction of military defense; or, as at Ferrara, in strengthening the fortifications of land and harbor; or, as at any of these cities, in the selection and execution of mural decorations for palaces and public buildings, and of scenery for pageants and plays—no matter what the occasion, the partnership was profitable.

The service of scholarship to art which resulted from this association requires no elaboration here. Without it, those frescoes of the early sixteenth century which still excite the wonder and admiration of the most cultivated would scarcely have been possible. Less clearly recognized is the service of mediaeval art to scholarship. There is, to be sure, a hint of this recognition in Castiglione's recommendation that the perfect courtier should also possess a knowledge of painting. His argument is buttressed, of course, with reference to the high regard in which painters were held by leaders of antiquity like Alexander, but it is also supported by some shrewd observations of his own:

> ... And do not marvel [he writes] that I desire this art, which today may seem to savor of the artisan and little to befit the gentleman ... which besides being very worthy in itself, is of great utility, and especially in war for drawing places, sites, rivers, bridges, rocks, fortresses and the like; since however well we may keep them in memory (which is very difficult) we cannot show them to others.

Though one of the first to mention this function of art, Castiglione was by no means the first to notice it or to make use of it. Mention has already been made of the fact that on his campaigns in the Romagna, Caesar Borgia enjoyed the services of both Machiavelli and Leonardo da Vinci.

It is not a mere freak of genius that at Pavia, Padua, and Florence Leonardo was so much in the company of professors of medicine, mathematics, and the humanities. That association was occurring among less famous men at all of these centers, for the artists had developed their skill in the observation of visible phenomena to a point scarcely then imagined by professors of medicine or other scientists. With the help of mathematicians, the artists had been able so to extend their powers of observation and to record their results that many turned to them for instruction in precision and accuracy; and the development of printing afforded a medium through which such recorded observations could be quickly communicated to scholars in all parts of Europe.

This blending of talents undoubtedly helped to make possible a considerable advance in science and technology. The anatomical drawings of Leonardo da Vinci are now well known; and he is still accorded credit for having observed and recorded details of human anatomy not hitherto known to medical professors. Likewise the drawings of much lesser artists were destined to figure in the epoch-making work of Vesalius, student and professor at the University of Padua. Reference has been made elsewhere to the important work of Fracostoro in the diagnosis of disease, another product of learning combined with improved observation. It was at Padua from a newly printed book on the writings of ancient Greek astronomers that the young Polish scholar, Copernicus, received encouragement in formulating his heliocentric theory of our universe. It was also there and at Pisa that Galileo developed his telescope which was so instrumental in confirming the theory of Copernicus. How much that erratic genius, Paracelsus, gained from his stay at Padua and Ferrara may never be determined, but modern medicine, chemistry, and pharmacy all acknowledge a debt to him. This combination of talents is also seen in the work of that humble schoolmaster from north of the Alps whose first bid for wider fame was the composition of a Latin grammar. With the savings of several years of teaching, however, he went to Italy where, chiefly at Padua, he became interested in medicine and science. Circumstances brought him into contact with mining, about which he wrote a highly illustrated book—one that has become a landmark in the history of both mining and geology. This was Georgius Agricola, whose *De re metallica* was translated recently into English by Herbert and Lou Henry Hoover. Another example of this blending of talents in the sixteenth century is that of Conrad Genser, who turned from collecting words in many languages to collecting and describing plants and animals, eventually producing a work which was to remain standard almost to the time of Darwin. All of these works represent a distinct advance beyond the classical heritage. It is a temptation to dwell upon this connection of humanism with science, all the more so since historians of science are so loathe to acknowledge the connection, but these illustrations must be sufficient.

Thus, by the sixteenth century, the great centers of humanism, Pavia, Padua, and Pisa, had become the leading centers of learning in Europe, overshadowing even those great old universities, Paris, Bologna, and Oxford. The latter had already discovered that their hope of maintaining or regaining their position was somehow dependent upon the extent to which they took over the new learning. However, by this time the interest in it had increased so greatly that neither three nor even six universities could suffice to satisfy the demand. Humanism had spread to all parts of Europe bringing with it the establishment of new centers of learning under secular auspices. It had come, in fact, to be an accepted part of the intellectual interest of modern times.

Yet it is at this point, the sixteenth century, that the historian of humanism finds himself most deeply perplexed. The humanities have become accepted as the best means of education. Practically all secondary education employs them and all the older universities have been forced to yield them a place. Ariosto and Tasso, Rabelais and Montaigne, Vives and Ximenes, Copernicus, Georgius Agricola and Gesner are all products of humanistic education. Luther and Calvin are heavily indebted to it while Melancthon and the whole order of the Jesuits are even more fully influenced by it. Scholars trained in the humanities make important contributions not only in literature and philology but also in law and medicine, mathematics and astronomy, geography and geology, botany and zoology, technology of many kinds including the art and science of war, history, political science, philosophy, and theology, Catholic as well as Protestant. There appear to be no limits to the area of their inquiries, not even is theology omitted. While many confine their production to fields of special aptitude, many of them, like Gesner, apparently assume that all knowledge is the legitimate goal of the individual scholar. Nor is there at the end of that century much if any evidence of any serious quarrel about vested intellectual interests. True, there are serious objections to particular discoveries and the embattled religious groups strike out harshly at what they regard as heresy but apparently there is no longer objection to the theologian's interest in the humanities, or the humanist's interest in theology, nor to the interest of either in natural phenomena. This is all so contrary to the conventional description of either humanism or of the intellectual interests of the period as to require explanation.

One obvious explanation for the failure to note this peculiar character of intellectual activity in the sixteenth century is the possibility that the historian, like the newspaper editor, drops a subject when it loses "news value." Humanism having become so widely accepted by that time, may be taken for granted and historical attention devoted to other matters more controversial. Another explanation may lie in the fact that the mediaevalist who is interested in humanism usually closes his work about 1500 A.D. while the modern historian, who begins at that point, is so much more engrossed in the clash of religious, national, and economic groups that he dismisses humanism as soon as possible, usually confining his remarks to its early connection with the religious controversy. As a result this widening of humanistic interest has escaped his attention. For the present these conjectures for the historian's neglect of this phenomenon must suffice.

The fact that the interests of humanists or of scholars trained in the humanities should deploy over such a vast horizon of intellectual activity can be more readily explained. Instruction involved masterpieces of Greek and Latin literature. The brighter pupils quickly extended their reading beyond the immediate texts. By the time they reached the universities such students would be exploring a wide range of both Greek and Latin writings, young Gesner, for example, trying to explore all the writings of antiquity long before his university career was ended. The work of edition and translation had been going on for several centuries by this time. The more obvious classics had been so treated; there remained now only the more obscure to which the professional humanist or the advanced student could most profitably devote his attention. The latter included works of a technical nature concerned with the whole range of intellectual inquiry of antiquity that had been preserved.

The method of education, too, had certain marked advantages. In the first place, the necessity of translation prevented the hurried superficial satisfaction of interest which writings in the pupil's own tongue might have permitted. The pupil was thus compelled to mull over each word, phrase, and idea which the author of his textbook used. He was forced also to seek the idea of the author in the life about him and thus to discover the words in his own language which would most nearly express the thought of the author. Few educators today, in appraising the value of the study in foreign languages, have taken account of this important fact: that the pupil is learning at least as much about his own times as he is about the circumstances involved in the work of the author whom he is attempting to translate.

The use of ancient masterpieces as instructional material, therefore, had exceptional merit. They represented the highest achievements of two unusually highly developed civilizations. It is doubtful whether we have even today any more perfect laboratories for the study of human motivation than those afforded by the Acropolis and the Forum. Not that other centers, especially of modern times, do not offer as great an interplay of human motives and in even greater

History and the Humanities

abundance. The advantage of those earlier centers rests in the fact that life offered fewer distractions, the activities were confined to smaller areas and could, therefore, be more accurately observed. Furthermore, the activities of each of these centers were exposed for several centuries to the cumulative gaze of unusually sensitive observers, endowed with rare powers of intuition. Finally these observers were able in the course of the centuries to devise words with which to express even the most delicate shades of their perceptions. Poets, orators, historians, and philosophers vied with each other in effectiveness of expression which involved not only choice of words and form of composition but also rhythm and cadence of line and sentence. The most nearly perfect of such achievements of observation, thought, and expression were used for instruction in the humanities. The pupil who was thus forced to find in his own world and in his own language the most nearly equivalent idea and expression of it was therefore learning to understand his own world and time much more fully than he would otherwise have done. In other areas of human concern, the ancients were limited by their smaller geographical horizon but within those limits they had advanced very far. Few even among the teachers of the classics have emphasized the wide range of human experience which was touched upon in a curriculum such as the school of Vittorino and his followers offered. Nothing about man or nature seemed to pass unnoticed. The brighter the pupil, the more widely he read, the greater the range of human experience and thought he was able to uncover. The process automatically promoted and cultivated his observation of his own day and age. The scholars so trained were therefore quite ready by the sixteenth century to make important additions to knowledge in all the fields mentioned above.

It may be appropriate, before turning to the discussion of history in relation to the humanities, to summarize the conclusions regarding the humanities in history up to the end of the sixteenth century. The first conclusion I must draw is that humanism is no new phenomenon of the fourteenth century; and, furthermore, that there is little justification for the designation of the next two centuries as marking a different type of life to be described by the term Renaissance. Instead, it would be more correct to say that, after the days of the Roman Empire, whenever any number of people were sufficiently free from immediate concern about their livelihood and lives, the more intelligent regularly began to try to satisfy their curiosity about this world.

The most efficient means for the satisfaction of this curiosity, of course, was learning, or the study of books in which, then as now, were preserved mankind's accumulated experience and thought. The curious, therefore, turned to the writings of the ancients, not through any sentimental reverence for the past, but because the more recent writings were almost exclusively concerned with matters of religion, or the relation of this life to the life hereafter. Among the ancients, on the contrary, they found persons as curious about this life and this world as themselves, and persons much farther along the road to satisfying their desires in this direction.

The second conclusion which this historical survey seems to justify is that the humanists looked upon the study of the ancients, not as an end in itself, but very definitely as a means to an end. They were too deeply immersed in the affairs of their own day ever to detach themselves completely from such concerns. Had that been their wish, they could have found in the theological and scholastic writings a much more satisfactory means of psychological escape. They esteemed the ancients so highly precisely because they found in them so much applicable to their own affairs. Had they been able to satisfy their needs as fully and as well through more recent writings either in mediaeval Latin or in the vernacular, it is quite conceivable that there would have been no classical revival. The rapidity with which they turned to the translation of the ancient writings and to the composition of works in the vernacular strongly confirms such conjecture. This would also suggest that the more nearly they were able to obtain what they wanted to know in their own language, the less inclined they would be to trouble to learn the ancient languages.

A third conclusion is that the Latin and Greek classics continued to be studied long after the demands of intellectual curiosity could be satisfied even more fully in the vernacular languages because they were believed to be a superior means of education. This position they held up until our own time. Whether the humanities have advanced in the vernacular beyond the best of the ancients sufficiently to make the further study of Latin and Greek unnecessary except for those whose professions require that knowledge must be discussed by others. As an historian, I must content myself with the observation that there are still many in the new world as well as the old who prefer the medium of Latin and Greek.

V

Having arrived at this summary of the nature of "humanism" and the Renaissance, we may now proceed, in light of it, to a brief consideration of the relation existing between history and the humanities. History was in ancient times one of the humanities and was included as such in the curriculum of the schools. Quintillian discusses its place in education at considerable length. The church fathers, though discarding the use of the classical historians, found history important for their needs and accordingly rewrote the history of the earlier times to suit their purposes. The example which they set was followed throughout the early Middle Ages. History continued to be written as well as read. For the most part it consisted of meager chronicles of events usually explained as the operation of God's will on earth. In those periods when secular curiosity found greater opportunity, the historical writing was usually expanded with a corresponding effort to probe the human factors as well. During the "Renaissance" of the twelfth century such writers as John of Salisbury and William of Tyre moved far in this direction. During the thirteenth century there was considerable writing of history in the vernacular in which the human factors received a similar emphasis. The influence of classical models is especially notable in the several periods of "Renaissance."

For the humanists of the so-called Renaissance history shared with poetry, oratory, and philosophy a leading place among the humanities. Caesar, Livy, and Sallust, Herodotus, Xenophon and Thucydides, as well as Plutarch and Aulus Gellius were widely read. There is scarcely a humanist of the period who does not reveal some acquaintance with the historians of antiquity and the writings of the period show to what use this knowledge was put. When their system of education became formulated by Vittorino and others history was given a prominent place in the curriculum. This arrangement met with the approval of Castiglione who says of his perfect courtier,

> I would have him more than passably accomplished in those studies that are called the humanities, and conversant not only with the Latin language but with the Greek for the sake of the many different things that have been admirably written therein. Let him be well versed in the poets and not less in the orators and historians.

The ancient historians served as models of literary style, as sources of illuminating illustrations and allusion, as aids in the observation and appraisal of human affairs, as sources for standards of human conduct and practical guidance. The way in which they wrote was thought to lend dignity as well as interest to the actors and events described, and both style and substance were therefore considered important. Historians, in other words, were regarded by the humanists as being both entertaining and instructive—a point of view often overlooked by textbook writers today.

Perhaps an illustration from the beginning and end of the Italian Renaissance will best reveal the effect of the study of ancient historians upon the humanists who wrote history. Leonardo Bruni composed his history of Florence in Latin, conscious that "Rome had become celebrated through illustrious writers—especially Livy—whom she produced and who will be famous through all the ages. And though the deeds of the Florentines may not be compared with those of the Romans, he [Bruni] endeavored to the best of his powers to celebrate their fame without departing from the truth." It must be admitted, however, that Bruni was more successful in celebrating their fame than in recounting the true record of their past. By his pen, Florentine burghers were made to move along to the music of Livy's sonorous sentences their destiny to fulfil. The Florentines, however, were thrilled by the result and Leonardo was rewarded with a state funeral and one of the finest tombs that sculpture could then contrive.

Nearly a century later, Machiavelli wrote his history of Florence. He was even more deeply read in the classical historians than Leonardo Bruni, but he wrote his history in Italian. Nor was he less conscious of the need for style or even for elegance in historical writing, but his own efforts followed no one classical model closely. Rather, his was a matured style reflecting many sources, but woven together in a manner distinctive of Machiavelli himself. Likewise, his work revealed a better command of language, a more diligent search for the truth, a more penetrating insight into motives, and a keener understanding of the connection between events. He had learned from the ancients what to observe and how; and these lessons he applied, with improvements, to his own times. The fruits of his study appear even more clearly in his more famous work, *The Prince*. As a recognition of his talent, he and another Florentine historian, Guicciardini, were entrusted with the task of planning for the defense of Florence against the armies of Charles V.

A further step in the development of history appears in the work of another humanistic scholar just after the close of the sixteenth century. This is the *De jure belli et pacis* of Hugo Grotius. His remarkable abilities were recognized by the Dutch States-General which appointed him official historiographer when he was but twenty years of age. The work for which he is especially famous grew out of the application of history to a specific problem of the day and is commonly regarded as the foundation of international law.

The development of history from Bruni to Machiavelli and Grotius closely paralleled the development of other interests of humanists. There was the same close study of the ancients, the same application of what they learned to the problems of their own time, the sharpened powers of observation, the more comprehensive outlook upon their immediate problem, improved skill in focusing both learning, observation, and thought upon an immediate problem and the effective expression of the results of this effort. The works of Machiavelli and Grotius mark a great advance not only over earlier mediaeval writers in history but, in important respects, over those written by the ancients.

The improvement thus made in history can by no means, however, be ascribed to the study of ancient historians alone. The keener appreciation of human motivation was derived quite as much if not more from the reading of the classical poets, orators, and philosophers. The critical analysis of earlier works, whether mediaeval or ancient, was derived as much from philological studies of the more purely literary humanists like Valla and Scaliger as from the historians. Just as those interested in nature were assisted in observing visible phenomena by mathematicians and artists, so in these more subtle areas of human affairs the historian learned from all the other humanities. It was their help which facilitated the penetration of the atmosphere of emotion in which the affairs of men were usually transacted. Historians like Machiavelli and Grotius brought to bear upon their immediate problems equipment drawn from a wide range of learning, observation, and thought. The skill with which they presented their solution of the problems was similarly derived.

Summarizing, then, the debt of history to the other humanities, it is fair, I think, to say that, by the sixteenth century, history had advanced in three particulars: in a fuller comprehension of human motivation in the conduct of public affairs, in a more critical use of documents, and in a more precise and effective recording of events.

Since the so-called Renaissance, history, like other subjects, has continued to develop and much of its enrichment now, as then, has come from other fields. Thanks to the advance in knowledge of nature during the seventeenth and eighteenth centuries history has been able to penetrate into that area of causation which remained veiled to the ancients under the general title of Fate. Thus, the influence of the natural or physical environment has become a recognized factor in human affairs and, with the advent of humanitarianism in the eighteenth century, the part played by the common man has been more emphasized. Since that time, leadership in human affairs has been increasingly appraised in terms of the willingness of followers to be led. In the nineteenth century, both science and humanitarianism continued to advance and, with them, the idea of scientific evolution began also to affect the study of history. Oddly enough the growing recognition of the importance of business with its paraphernalia of statistics was to join with the humanitarian ideology of class conflict in emphasizing the importance of those traits and tastes which men hold in common. Most recently psychology has undertaken to apply scientific methods to the study of human motivation and in so doing has supplied history with yet another angle of approach to its problems.

The end result of all this varied enrichment has been at times somewhat confusing, both in terms of the organization and of the content of history.

History once was the only study of man and society, but has been forced to expand and entrust to its offspring, the social sciences, important areas of its previous concern. This modern expansion has raised important questions in academic organization. What was once a single subject has become a group of subjects, even a whole division of the college curriculum. On the whole, the academic world has accepted this expansion of history into a division of social science without controversy or even serious debate. Recently, however, when the University of Chicago sought to set up definite divisions of social sciences and the humanities, history found itself in an unhappy position. By implication, at least, the social sciences were not regarded as humanities. This was a conclusion which history was not prepared to admit. The debate raged for months, and the final decision, or at least one of the final decisions, was that the department of history belonged to both divisions. In a general way, those members of the department who were primarily interested in recent history were regarded as more closely identified with the social sciences, while those concerned with the earlier periods were deemed more closely associated with the humanities. Circumstances at Chicago required some sort of decision but the question still remains unsettled and concerns the whole academic world.

Furthermore, under the influence of all these modern intellectual movements history has at times seemed to abandon the gains derived from the humanistic development of the Renaissance. Overemphasis upon the determinative influence of physical environment did apparently belittle the importance of man with which the humanists were so much concerned. Fascinated by the forces of nature, many historians completely overlooked the fact that individuals living in the same regions were behaving in widely different ways. Naturalism become ideological was to be quite as objectionable to humanism as the latter was thought to have been to scholasticism.

Likewise as the study of science led to the formulation of laws cosmic in scope, scholars in other fields were encouraged to hope that they, too, might be able to find similar laws in their own areas of research. In this expectation, they sought to take over what appeared to them to be the successful methods of scientific research. Objectivity was deemed to be one of these methods. To attain objectivity, historians ruthlessly stripped the materials of history of all subjective elements, moral or aesthetic. The quest was for bare facts, the more the better. These facts accumulated in imposing mass were grouped about institutions, political, social, and economic; and, thus grouped, they were somehow expected to "speak for themselves" and almost automatically to yield laws, or at least principles, comparable to those of science. There was little place in the vast masses of so-called fact resulting from this effort for either the feelings, hopes, or wishes of man and very little for his thoughts. Any regard for style in such compilations was, of course, superfluous.

The naïve adaptation of scientific evolution, which scarcely recognizes the development of a single new species in less than the last fifty million years, to the affairs of man, whose recorded history extends over little more than the last three thousand years, had results equally abhorrent to the humanities. It led, as Bury has remarked, to an illusion of progress under whose influence everything in the present assumed all the virtues of natural selection. This conception automatically belittled the thoughts and achievements of men in the past. Under such an hypothesis, Jefferson, Hamilton, and Franklin could only be regarded as shoulder high, Virgil and Cicero as mere pygmies, Plato and Aristotle as even more microscopic, while poor Homer was left floundering among the amoebae. Surely the scientist, no less than the humanist, must have shuddered at this misuse of his theory.

Equally unpalatable were the extreme effects of humanitarian and capitalistic influences upon writers of history. Only matters common to mankind were deemed valuable. Only facts which could be expressed quantitatively, analyzed statistically, and charted graphically seemed to matter. Both mass production and mass approval were thought to depend upon these factors and they were therefore determinative. Unusual individuals and uncommon traits of common men disappeared in the statistical hopper as of no significance. It is one of the paradoxes of life that some scholars should have sought to attain personal distinction by urging acceptance of such an interpretation of society.

As yet only a few professional historians have allowed themselves to be swept off their feet by the contributions of scientific psychology. There have, however, been some historians, more of them amateur than professional, who have attempted to rewrite not only biographies but also episodes and even to explain such phenomena as social movements and political leadership in terms of Freudian complexes. As the contributions of psychologists multiply, however, it is conceivable that more of our profession will become as fascinated by them as they have by the contributions of other fields of scholarship. For the momentary sway of a newly grasped concept is no less overwhelming than the lure of a single explanation for highly complex phenomena. Then the humanities will have further cause for grief.

The very recognition of these excesses of historical scholarship in modern times is itself evidence of their transitory character. They have not all been eradicated as yet. Indeed they still flourish in varying measure among the several social sciences. But the trend is, I believe, definitely away from their worst effects. Only a few years ago, members of the historical professions seemed much more fascinated by test-tubes and telescopes, millimeters and micrometers, slide-rules and comptometers, business charts and statistical formulae, machinery and technology than they do today. While still recognizing the importance of such aids in understanding the affairs of men, the majority of historical scholars appear now to understand their limitations as well. That is, historians have come to recognize the fact that, however many persons are affected by technological devices, all such devices are made and must be operated by men. They have discovered also that, however vast the body of facts which they collect, into whatever graphic symbols these facts may be compressed, decisions regarding their use must be made by individuals. They have learned, too, that however much men may have in common and however important these common characteristics may be, the dynamic quality of society is derived from the individual who sets the mass in motion or determines its direction, and is therefore distinctive. Even the equalitarian social experiment in Russia, for example, can scarcely be comprehended without reference to its leaders—a fact becoming increasingly apparent to the Russians themselves. However important natural forces and mass movements may appear, human motivation and leadership have not ceased to be vital factors in the affairs of society. They have come to recognize the fact that the three or four thousand years of documented history are too brief to assure a definite evolutionary trend, but have gained from the experience a clear conception of development in human affairs even though the direction of that development may at times quite reverse itself. And along with this wider understanding, members of the historical professions have learned that bare facts do not speak for themselves. They have learned again that if their findings are to be effectively communicated to others these findings must be expressed in language best suited to the purpose.

It is unnecessary to turn to professors of ancient or mediaeval history for confirmation of the trend toward a more humanistic balance in the study and writing of history. None has pointed out more frequently the dangers which the historian risks from excessive attachment to any modern intellectual ideology than has Carl Becker, some of whose pertinent essays were recently published under the title *Everyman His Own Historian*. None has summed up these dangers more vigorously than has Beard in those remarkable first chapters of his *Nature of the Social Sciences*. His emphatic assertion of the paramount importance of the humanistic element in the historical sciences derives peculiar force from his long and wide intimacy with all the social sciences. Few writers have defined the humanistic elements of history more clearly than has Cheyney in the *Encyclopedia of the Social Sciences*. And few have exemplified the humanistic elements in the writing of history more gracefully than has Dodd in his major work which is just now appearing off the press. All of these men are primarily concerned with modern events and such instances might be greatly multiplied from the writings of other modern historians and social scientists whose fame is not yet so firmly established.

These and other historical scholars do not, however, intend to sacrifice any of the gains secured by the intellectual advance of the last three centuries. They intend to include in their thinking the recognizable influence of nature on the affairs of men and of the masses on those who lead them. They may even continue to use some of the convenient symbols devised by business to express large aggregates of fact briefly. And if and when psychology arrives at a more precise identification of individual and group motivation, they will, doubtless, also make use of that advance. They will employ all of these variant avenues to knowledge in the hope of approaching more closely to the truth of human affairs—a service which from the beginning history was supposed to render to the other humanities. For in the effort to record and explain the long story of human development, history must continue to seek, wherever it may be found, the language best fitted to convey the thoughts, acts, and feelings of men. It must continue to take into account all the ethical and aesthetic as well as material elements involved in any situation. To discharge these responsibilities, it must, in the future, as in the past, rely upon the other humanities which, I presume, have also made progress.

This, then, I take to be the true meaning of the humanities in the process of education: that they are not ends in themselves, not closed formulae within which the mind is confined, but means capable of endless improvement, and the best means of inducting youth into an understanding of the world. In that sense, therefore, humanism and the Renaissance did not come to an end in the sixteenth century, even less than they began in the fourteenth.

THE HISTORY OF ART AS A HUMANISTIC DISCIPLINE
By ERWIN PANOFSKY

THE HISTORY OF ART AS A
HUMANISTIC DISCIPLINE

I

NINE days before his death Immanuel Kant was visited by his physician. Old, ill and nearly blind, he rose from his chair and stood trembling with weakness and muttering unintelligible words. Finally his faithful companion realized that he would not sit down again until the visitor had taken a seat. This he did, and Kant then permitted himself to be helped to his chair and, after having regained some of his strength, said, "Das Gefühl für Humanität hat mich noch nicht verlassen"—"The sense of humanity has not yet left me."[1] The two men were moved almost to tears. For, though the word *Humanität* had come, in the eighteenth century, to mean little more than politeness or civility, it had, for Kant, a much deeper significance, which the circumstances of the moment served to emphasize: man's proud and tragic consciousness of self-approved and self-imposed principles, contrasting with his utter subjection to illness, decay and all that is implied in the word "mortality."

Historically the word *humanitas* has had two clearly distinguishable meanings, the first arising from a contrast between man and what is less than man; the second, between man and what is more. In the first case *humanitas* means a value, in the second a limitation.

The concept of *humanitas* as a value was formulated in the circle around the younger Scipio, with Cicero as its belated, yet most explicit spokesman. It meant the quality which

---

[1] E. A. C. Wasianski, *Immanuel Kant in seinen letzten Lebensjahren* (*Ueber Immanuel Kant*, 1804, Vol. III), reprinted in *Immanuel Kant, Sein Leben in Darstellungen von Zeitgenossen*, Deutsche Bibliothek, Berlin, 1912, p. 298.

distinguishes man, not only from animals, but also, and even more so, from him who belongs to the species *homo* without deserving the name of *homo humanus*; from the barbarian or vulgarian who lacks *pietas* and παιδεία—that is, respect for moral values and that gracious blend of learning and urbanity which we can only circumscribe by the discredited word "culture."

In the Middle Ages this concept was displaced by the consideration of humanity as being opposed to divinity rather than to animality or barbarism. The qualities commonly associated with it were therefore those of frailty and transience: *humanitas fragilis, humanitas caduca.*

Thus the Renaissance conception of *humanitas* had a twofold aspect from the outset. The new interest in the human being was based both on a revival of the classical antithesis between *humanitas* and *barbaritas,* or *feritas,* and on a survival of the mediaeval antithesis between *humanitas* and *divinitas.* When Marsilio Ficino defines man as a "rational soul participating in the intellect of God, but operating in a body," he defines him as the one being that is both autonomous and finite. And Pico's famous "speech," "On the Dignity of Man," is anything but a document of paganism. Pico says that God placed man in the center of the universe so that he might be conscious of where he stands, and therefore free to decide "where to turn." He does not say that man *is* the center of the universe, not even in the sense of the classical phrase, "man the measure of all things."

It is from this ambivalent conception of *humanitas* that humanism was born. It is not so much a movement as an attitude which can be defined as the conviction of the dignity of man, based on both the insistence on human values (rationality and freedom) and the acceptance of human limitations (fallibility and frailty); from this two postulates result—responsibility and tolerance.

The History of Art

Small wonder that this attitude has been attacked from two opposite camps whose common aversion to the ideas of responsibility and tolerance has recently aligned them in a united front. Entrenched in one of these camps are those who deny human values: the determinists, whether they believe in divine, physical or social predestination, the authoritarians, and those "insectolatrists" who profess the all-importance of the hive, whether the hive be called group, class, nation or race. In the other camp are those who deny human limitations in favor of some sort of intellectual or political libertinism, such as aestheticists, vitalists, intuitionists and hero-worshipers. From the point of view of determinism, the humanist is either a lost soul or an ideologist. From the point of view of authoritarianism, he is either a heretic or a revolutionary (or a counter-revolutionary). From the point of view of "insectolatry," he is a useless individualist. And from the point of view of libertinism he is a timid bourgeois.

Erasmus of Rotterdam, the humanist *par excellence,* is a typical case in point. The church suspected and ultimately rejected the writings of this man who had said: "Perhaps the spirit of Christ is more largely diffused than we think, and there are many in the community of saints who are not in our calendar." The adventurer Ulrich von Hutten despised his ironical scepticism and his unheroic love of tranquillity. And Luther, who insisted that "no man has power to think anything good or evil, but everything occurs in him by absolute necessity," was incensed by a belief which manifested itself in the famous phrase: "What is the use of man as a totality [that is, of man endowed with both a body and a soul], if God would work in him as a sculptor works in clay, and might just as well work in stone?"[2]

[2] For the quotations from Luther and Erasmus of Rotterdam see the excellent monograph *Humanitas Erasmiana* by R. Pfeiffer, Studien der Bibliothek Warburg, XXII, 1931. It is significant that Erasmus and Luther rejected judicial or fatalistic astrology for totally different reasons: Erasmus refused to believe that human destiny depends on the unalterable movements of the celestial bodies, because

II

The humanist, then, rejects authority. But he respects tradition. Not only does he respect it, he looks upon it as upon something real and objective which has to be studied and, if necessary, reinstated: *"nos vetera instauramus, nova non prodimus,"* as Erasmus puts it.

The Middle Ages accepted and developed rather than studied and restored the heritage of the past. They copied classical works of art and used Aristotle and Ovid much as they copied and used the works of contemporaries. They made no attempt to interpret them from an archaeological, philological or "critical," in short, from an historical, point of view. For, if human existence could be thought of as a means rather than an end, how much less could the records of human activity be considered as values in themselves.[3]

In mediaeval scholasticism there is, therefore, no basic distinction between natural science and what we call the human-

---

such a belief would amount to a denial of human free will and responsibility; Luther, because it would amount to a restriction of the omnipotence of God. Luther therefore believed in the significance of *terata*, such as eight-footed calves, etc., which God can cause to appear at irregular intervals.

[3] Some historians seem to be unable to recognize continuities and distinctions at the same time. It is undeniable that humanism, and the entire Renaissance movement, did not spring forth like Athena from the head of Zeus. But the fact that Lupus of Ferrières emended classical texts, that Hildebert of Lavardin had a strong feeling for the ruins of Rome, that the French and English scholars of the twelfth century revived classical philosophy and mythology, and that Marbod of Rennes wrote a fine pastoral poem on his small country estate, does not mean that their outlook was identical with that of Petrarch, let alone of Ficino or Erasmus. No mediaeval man could see the civilization of antiquity as a phenomenon complete in itself and historically detached from the contemporary world; as far as I know, mediaeval Latin has no equivalent to the humanistic *"antiquitas"* or *"sacrosancta vetustas."* And just as it was impossible for the Middle Ages to elaborate a system of perspective based on the realization of a fixed distance between the eye and the object, so it was equally impossible for this period to evolve an idea of historical disciplines based on the realization of a fixed distance between the present and the classical past. See E. Panofsky and F. Saxl, "Classical Mythology in Mediaeval Art," *Studies of the Metropolitan Museum*, IV, 2, 1933, pp. 228 ff., particularly pp. 263 ff., and recently the interesting article by W. S. Heckscher, "Relics of Pagan Antiquity in Mediaeval Settings," *Journal of the Warburg Institute*, I, 1937, pp. 204 ff.

ities, *studia humaniora,* to quote again an Erasmian phrase. The practice of both, so far as it was carried on at all, remained within the framework of what was called philosophy. From the humanistic point of view, however, it became reasonable, and even inevitable, to distinguish, within the realm of creation, between the sphere of *nature* and the sphere of *culture,* and to define the former with reference to the latter, *i.e.* nature as the whole world accessible to the senses, except for the *records left by man.*

Man is indeed the only animal to leave records behind him, for he is the only animal whose products "recall to mind" an idea distinct from their material existence. Other animals use signs and contrive structures, but they use signs without "perceiving the relation of signification,"[4] and they contrive structures without perceiving the relation of construction.

To perceive the relation of signification is to separate the idea of the concept to be expressed from the means of expression. And to perceive the relation of construction is to separate the idea of the function to be fulfilled from the means of fulfilling it. A dog announces the approach of a stranger by a bark quite different from that by which he makes known his wish to go out. But he will not use this particular bark to convey the idea that a stranger *has* called during the absence of his master. Much less will an animal, even if it were physically able to do so, as apes indubitably are, ever attempt to represent anything in a picture. Beavers build dams. But they are unable, so far as we know, to separate the very complicated actions involved from a premeditated *plan* which might be laid down in a drawing instead of being materialized in logs and stones.

Man's signs and structures are records because, or rather in so far as, they express ideas separated from, yet realized by, the processes of signaling and building. These records have

[4] See J. Maritain, "Sign and Symbol," *Journal of the Warburg Institute,* I, 1937, pp. 1 *ff.*

therefore the quality of *emerging from the stream of time,* and it is precisely in this respect that they are studied by the humanist. He is, fundamentally, an *historian.*

The scientist, too, deals with human records, namely with the works of his predecessors. But he deals with them not as something to be investigated, but as something which helps him to investigate. In other words, he is interested in records not in so far as they emerge from the stream of time, but in so far as they are absorbed in it. If a modern scientist reads Newton or Leonardo da Vinci in the original, he does so not as a scientist, but as a man interested in the history of science and therefore of human civilization in general. In other words, he does it as a *humanist,* for whom the works of Newton or Leonardo da Vinci have an autonomous meaning and a lasting value. From the humanistic point of view, human records do not age.

Thus, while science endeavors to transform the chaotic variety of natural phenomena into what may be called a *cosmos of nature,* the humanities endeavor to transform the chaotic variety of human records into what may be called a *cosmos of culture.*

There are, in spite of all the differences in subject and procedure, some very striking analogies between the methodical problems to be coped with by the scientist, on the one hand, and by the humanist, on the other.[5]

In both cases the process of investigation seems to begin with observation. But both the observer of a natural phenomenon and the examiner of a record are not only confined to the limits of their range of vision and to the available material; in directing their attention to *certain* objects they obey,

---

[5] See E. Wind, *Das Experiment und die Metaphysik,* Tübingen, 1934, and *idem,* "Some Points of Contact between History and Natural Science," *Philosophy and History, Essays presented to Ernst Cassirer,* Oxford, 1936, pp. 255 ff. (with a very instructive discussion of the relationship between phenomena, instruments and the observer, on the one hand, and historical facts, documents and the historian, on the other).

knowingly or not, a principle of pre-selection dictated by a theory in the case of the scientist and by a general historical conception in the case of the humanist. It may be true that "nothing is in the mind except what was in the senses"; but it is at least equally true that much is in the senses without ever penetrating into the mind. We are chiefly affected by that which we *allow* to affect us; and just as natural science involuntarily selects what it calls the phenomena, the humanities involuntarily select what they call the historical facts. Thus the humanities have gradually widened their cultural cosmos and in some measure have shifted the accents of their interests. Even he who instinctively sympathizes with the simple definition of the humanities as "Latin and Greek" and considers this definition as essentially valid as long as we use such ideas and expressions as, for instance, "idea" and "expression"—even he has to admit that it has become a trifle narrow.

Furthermore, the world of the humanities is determined by a cultural theory of relativity, comparable to that of the physicists; and since the cosmos of culture is so much smaller than the cosmos of nature, cultural relativity prevails within terrestrial dimensions, and was observed at a much earlier date.

Every historical concept is obviously based on the categories of space and time. The records, and what they imply, have to be *dated* and *located*. But it turns out that these two acts are in reality two aspects of one. If I date a picture about 1400, this statement would be meaningless if I could not indicate *where* it could have been produced at that date; conversely, if I ascribe a picture to the Florentine school, I must be able to tell *when* it could have been produced in that school. The cosmos of culture, like the cosmos of nature, is a spatio-temporal structure. The year 1400 means something different in Venice from what it means in Florence, to say nothing of Augsburg, or Russia, or Constantinople. Two historical phenomena are simultaneous, or have a determinable temporal relation to each other, only in so far as they can be related within one "frame of reference," in the absence of which the very concept of simultaneity would be as meaningless in history as it would in physics. If we knew by some concatenation of circumstances that a certain negro sculpture had been executed in 1510, it would be meaningless to say that it was "contemporaneous" with Michelangelo's Sistine ceiling.[6]

Finally, the *succession of steps* by which the material is organized into a natural or cultural cosmos is analogous, and the same is true of the methodical problems implied by this process. The first step is, as has already been mentioned, the observation of natural phenomena and the examination of human records. Then the records have to be "decoded" and interpreted, as must the "messages from nature" received by the observer. Finally the results have to be classified and coordinated into a coherent system that "makes sense."

Now we have seen that even the selection of the material *for* observation and examination is predetermined, to some extent, by a theory, or by a general historical conception. This is even more evident in the procedure itself, as every step made towards the system that "makes sense" presupposes not only the preceding but also the succeeding ones.

When the scientist observes a phenomenon he uses *instruments* which are themselves subject to the laws of nature which he wants to explore. When the humanist examines a record he uses *documents* which are themselves produced in the course of the process which he wants to investigate.

Let us suppose that I find in the archives of a small town in the Rhineland a contract dated 1471, and complemented by records of payments, by which the local painter "Johannes *qui et* Frost" was commissioned to execute for the church of St. James in that town an altarpiece with

---

[6] See, *e.g.*, E. Panofsky, "Ueber die Reihenfolge der vier Meister von Reims" (Appendix), *Jahrbuch für Kunstwissenschaft*, II, 1927, pp. 77 *ff*.

the Nativity in the center and Saints Peter and Paul on the wings; and let us further suppose that I find in the Church of St. James an altarpiece corresponding to this contract. That would be a case of documentation as good and simple as we could possibly hope to encounter, much better and simpler than if we had to deal with an "indirect" source such as a letter, or a description in a chronicle, biography, diary, or poem. Yet several questions would present themselves.

The document may be an original, a copy or a forgery. If it is a copy, it may be a faulty one, and even if it is an original, some of the data may be wrong. The altarpiece in turn may be the one referred to in the contract; but it is equally possible that the original monument was destroyed during the iconoclastic riots of 1535 and was replaced by an altarpiece showing the same subjects, but executed around 1550 by a painter from Antwerp.

To arrive at any degree of certainty we would have to "check" the document against other documents of similar date and provenance, and the altarpiece against other paintings executed in the Rhineland around 1470. But here two difficulties arise.

First, "checking" is obviously impossible without our knowing *what* to "check"; we would have to *single out* certain features or criteria such as some forms of script, or some technical terms used in the contract, or some formal or iconographic peculiarities manifested in the altarpiece. But since we cannot analyze what we do not understand, our examination turns out to presuppose decoding and interpretation.

Secondly, the material *against* which we check our problematic case is in itself no better authenticated than the problematic case in hand. Taken individually, any other signed and dated monument is just as doubtful as the altarpiece ordered from "Johannes *qui et* Frost" in 1471. (It is self-evident that a signature on a picture can be, and often is, just as unreliable as a document connected with a picture.) It is only on the basis of a whole group or class of data that we can decide whether our altarpiece was stylistically and iconographically "possible" in the Rhineland around 1470. But classification obviously presupposes the idea of a whole to which the classes belong—in other words, the general historical conception which we try to build up from our individual cases.

However we may look at it, the *beginning* of our investigation always seems to presuppose the *end,* and the *documents* which should explain the monuments are just as enigmatical as the monuments themselves. It is quite possible that a technical term in our contract is a ἅπαξ λεγόμενον which can only be explained by this one altarpiece; and what an artist has said about his own works must always be interpreted in the light of the works themselves. We are apparently faced with a hopeless vicious circle. Actually it is what the philosophers call an "organic situation."[7] Two legs without a body cannot walk, and a body without legs cannot walk either, yet a man can walk. It is true that the individual monuments and documents can only be examined, interpreted and classified in the light of a general historical concept, while at the same time this general historical concept can only be built up on individual monuments and documents; just as the understanding of natural phenomena and the use of scientific instruments depends on a general physical theory and vice versa. Yet this situation is by no means a permanent deadlock. Every discovery of an unknown historical fact, and every new interpretation of a known one, will either "fit in" with the prevalent general conception, and thereby corroborate and enrich it, or else it will entail a subtle, or even a fundamental change in the prevalent general conception, and

[7] I am indebted for this term to Professor T. M. Greene.

thereby throw new light on all that has been known before. In both cases the "system that makes sense" operates as a consistent yet elastic organism, comparable to a living animal as opposed to its single limbs; and what is true of the relationship between monuments, documents and a general historical concept in the humanities is evidently equally true of the relationship between phenomena, instruments and theory in the natural sciences.

III

I have referred to the altarpiece of 1471 as a "monument" and to the contract as a "document"; that is to say, I have considered the altarpiece as the object of investigation, or "primary material," and the contract as an instrument of investigation, or "secondary material." In doing this I have spoken as an art-historian. For a palaeographer or an historian of law, the contract would be the "monument," or "primary material," and both may use pictures for documentation.

Unless a scholar is exclusively interested in what is called "events" (in which case he would consider all the available records as "secondary material" by means of which he might reconstruct the "events"), everyone's "monuments" are everyone else's "documents," and vice versa. In practical work we are even compelled actually to annex "monuments" rightfully belonging to our colleagues. Many a work of art has been interpreted by a philologist or by an historian of medicine; and many a text has been interpreted, and could only have been interpreted, by an historian of art.

An art-historian, then, is a humanist whose "primary material" consists of those records which have come down to us in the form of works of art. But what is a work of art?

A work of art is not always created *exclusively* for the purpose of being enjoyed, or, to use a more scholarly expression, of being experienced aesthetically. Poussin's statement that "la fin de l'art est la délectation" was quite a revolutionary one,[8] for earlier writers had always insisted that art, however enjoyable, was also, in some manner, useful. But a work of art always *has* aesthetic significance (not to be confused with aesthetic value): whether or not it serves some practical purpose, and whether it is good or bad, it *demands* to be experienced aesthetically.

It is possible to experience every object, natural or man-made, aesthetically. We do this, to express it as simply as possible, when we just look at it (or listen to it) without relating it, intellectually or emotionally, to anything outside of itself. When a man looks at a tree from the point of view of a carpenter, he will associate it with the various uses to which he might put the wood; and when he looks at it from the point of view of an ornithologist he will associate it with the birds that might nest in it. When a man at a horse race watches the animal on which he has put his money, he will associate its performance with his desire that it may win. Only he who simply and wholly abandons himself to the object of his perception will experience it aesthetically.[9]

Now, when confronted with a *natural* object, it is an exclusively personal matter whether or not we choose to experience it aesthetically. A man-made object, however, either *demands* or *does not demand* to be so experienced, for it has what the

---

[8] A. Blunt, "Poussin's Notes on Painting," *Journal of the Warburg Institute*, I, 1937, pp. 344 ff., claims (p. 349) that Poussin's "La fin de l'art est la délectation" was more or less "mediaeval," because "the theory of *delectatio* as the sign by which beauty is recognized is the key of all St. Bonaventura's aesthetic, and it may well be from there, probably by means of some populariser, that Poussin drew the definition." However, even if the wording of Poussin's phrase was influenced by a mediaeval source, there is a great difference between the statement that *delectatio* is a *distinctive quality* of everything *beautiful*, whether man-made or natural, and the statement that *delectatio* is the *end* ("*fin*") of *art*.

[9] See M. Geiger, "Beiträge zur Phänomenologie des aesthetischen Genusses," *Jahrbuch für Philosophie*, I, Part 2, 1922, pp. 567 ff. Furthermore, E. Wind, *Aesthetischer und kunstwissenschaftlicher Gegenstand*, Diss. phil. Hamburg, 1923, partly reprinted as "Zur Systematik der künstlerischen Probleme," *Zeitschrift für Aesthetik und allgemeine Kunstwissenschaft*, XVIII, 1925, pp. 438 ff.

scholastics call an *"intention."* Should I choose, as I might well do, to experience the redness of a traffic light aesthetically, instead of associating it with the idea of stepping on my brakes, I should act against the "intention" of the traffic light.

Those man-made objects which *do not* demand to be experienced aesthetically, are commonly called "practical," and may be divided into two classes: *vehicles of communication,* and *tools* or *apparatuses.* A vehicle of communication is "intended" to transmit a concept. A tool or apparatus is "intended" to fulfil a function (which function, in turn, may be the production or transmission of communications, as is the case with a typewriter or with the previously mentioned traffic light).

Most of the objects which do demand to be experienced aesthetically, that is to say, works of art, also belong in one of these two classes. A poem or an historical painting is, in a sense, a vehicle of communication; the Pantheon and the Milan candlesticks are, in a sense, apparatuses; and Michelangelo's tombs of Lorenzo and Giuliano de'Medici are, in a sense, both. But I have to say "in a sense," because there is this difference: in the case of what might be called a "mere vehicle of communication" and a "mere apparatus," the intention is definitely fixed on the *idea* of the work, namely, on the meaning to be transmitted, or on the function to be fulfilled. In the case of a work of art, the interest in the *idea* is *balanced,* and may even be *eclipsed,* by an interest in *form.*

However, the element of "form" is present in every object without exception, for every object consists of matter and form; and there is no way of determining with scientific precision to what extent, in a given case, this element of form bears the emphasis. Therefore one cannot, and should not, attempt to define the precise moment at which a vehicle of communication or an apparatus begins to be a work of art. If I write to a friend to ask him to dinner, my letter is primarily a communication. But the more I shift the emphasis to the form of my script, the more nearly does it become a work of calligraphy; and the more I emphasize the form of my language (I could even go so far as to invite him by a sonnet), the more nearly does it become a work of literature or poetry.

Where the sphere of practical objects ends, and that of "art" begins, depends, then, on the "intention" of the creators. This "intention" cannot be absolutely determined. In the first place, "intentions" are, *per se,* incapable of being defined with scientific precision. In the second place, the "intentions" of those who produce objects are conditioned by the standards of their period and environment. Classical taste demanded that private letters, legal speeches and the shields of heroes should be "artistic" (with the possible result of what might be called fake beauty), while modern taste demands that architecture and ash-trays should be "functional" (with the possible result of what might be called fake efficiency).[10] Finally

[10] "Functionalism" means, strictly speaking, not the introduction of a new aesthetic principle, but a narrower delimitation of the aesthetic sphere. When we prefer the modern steel helmet to the shield of Achilles, or feel that the "intention" of a legal speech should be definitely focused on the subject matter and should not be shifted to the form ("more matter with less *art,*" as Queen Gertrude rightly puts it), we merely demand that arms and legal speeches should not be treated as works of art, that is, aesthetically, but as practical objects, that is, technically. However, we have come to think of "functionalism" as a postulate instead of an interdict. The Classical and Renaissance civilizations, in the belief that a merely useful thing could not be "beautiful" ("non può essere bellezza e utilità," as Leonardo da Vinci puts it; see J. P. Richter, *The Literary Works of Leonardo da Vinci,* London, 1883, nr. 1445) are characterized by a tendency to extend the aesthetic attitude to such creations as are "naturally" practical; we have extended the technical attitude to such creations as are "naturally" artistic. This, too, is an infringement, and, in the case of "streamlining," art has taken its revenge. "Streamlining" was, originally, a genuine functional principle based on the results of scientific research on air resistance. Its legitimate sphere was therefore the field of fast-moving vehicles and of structures exposed to wind pressure of an extraordinary intensity. But when this special and truly technical device came to be interpreted as a general and aesthetic principle expressing the twentieth century ideal of "efficiency" ("streamline your mind!"), and was applied to arm chairs and cocktail shakers, it was felt that the original scientific streamline had to be "beautified"; and it was finally retransferred to where it rightfully belongs in a thoroughly non-functional form. As a result, we now have less often houses and furniture functionalized by engineers, than automobiles and railroad trains de-functionalized by designers.

our estimate of those "intentions" is inevitably influenced by our own attitude which in turn depends on our individual experiences as well as on our historical situation. We have all seen with our own eyes the transference of spoons and fetishes of African tribes from the museums of ethnology into art exhibitions.

One thing, however, is certain: the more the proportion of emphasis on "idea" and "form" approaches a state of equilibrium, the more eloquently will the work reveal what is called "content." *Content,* as opposed to subject matter, may be described in the words of Peirce as that which a work *betrays* but does not *parade*. It is the basic attitude of a nation, a period, a class, a religious or philosophical persuasion—all this unconsciously qualified by one personality, and condensed into one work. It is obvious that such an involuntary revelation will be obscured in proportion as either one of the two elements, idea or form, is voluntarily emphasized or suppressed. A spinning machine is perhaps the most impressive manifestation of a functional idea, and an "abstract" painting is perhaps the most expressive manifestation of pure form, but both have a minimum of content.

IV

In defining a work of art as a "man-made object demanding to be experienced aesthetically" we encounter for the first time a basic difference between the humanities and natural science. The scientist, dealing as he does with natural phenomena, can at once proceed to analyze them. The humanist, dealing as he does with human actions and creations, has to engage in a mental process of a synthetic and subjective character: he has mentally to *re-enact the actions* and to *re-create the creations*. It is in fact by this process that the real objects of the humanities come into being. For it is obvious that historians of philosophy or sculpture are concerned with books and statues not in so far as these books and sculptures exist materially, but in so far as they have a meaning. And it is equally obvious that this meaning can only be apprehended by re-producing, and thereby, quite literally, "realizing," the thoughts that are expressed in the books and the artistic conceptions that manifest themselves in the statues.

Thus the art-historian subjects his "material" to a rational archaeological analysis at times as meticulously exact, comprehensive and involved as any physical or astronomical research. But he constitutes his "material" by means of an intuitive aesthetic re-creation,[11] including the perception and appraisal of "quality," just as any "ordinary" person does when he or she looks at a picture or listens to a symphony.

How, then, is it possible to build up art-history as a respectable scholarly discipline, if its very objects come into being by an irrational and subjective process?

This question cannot be answered, of course, by referring to the scientific methods which have been, or may be, introduced into art-history. Devices such as chemical analysis of

[11] However, when speaking of "re-creation" it is important to emphasize the prefix "re." Works of art are both manifestations of artistic "intentions" and natural objects, sometimes difficult to isolate from their physical surroundings and always subject to the physical processes of aging. Thus, in experiencing a work of art aesthetically we perform two entirely different acts which, however, psychologically merge with each other into one *Erlebnis*: we build up our aesthetic object both by re-creating the work of art according to the "intention" of its maker, and by freely creating a set of aesthetic values comparable to those with which we endow a tree or a sunset. When abandoning ourselves to the impression of the weathered sculptures of Chartres, we cannot help enjoying their lovely mellowness and patina as an aesthetic value; but this value, which implies both the sensual pleasure in a peculiar play of light and color and the more sentimental delight in "age" and "genuineness," has nothing to do with the objective, or artistic, value with which the sculptures were invested by their makers. From the point of view of the Gothic stone-carvers the processes of aging were not merely irrelevant but positively undesirable: they tried to protect their statues by a coat of color which, had it been preserved in its original freshness, would probably spoil a good deal of our aesthetic enjoyment. As a private person, the art-historian is entirely justified in not destroying the psychological unity of *Alters-und-Echtheits-Erlebnis* and *Kunst-Erlebnis*. But as a "professional man" he has to separate, as far as possible, the re-creative experience of the intentional values imparted to the statue by the artist from the creative experience of the accidental values imparted to a piece of aged stone by the action of nature. And this separation is often not as easy as it might seem.

materials, X-rays, ultra-violet rays, infra-red rays and macrophotography are very helpful, but their use has nothing to do with the basic methodical problem. A statement to the effect that the pigments used in an allegedly mediaeval miniature were not invented before the nineteenth century may settle an art-historical *question,* but it is not an art-historical *statement*. Based as it is on chemical analysis plus the history of chemistry, it refers to the miniature not *qua* work of art but *qua* physical object, and may just as well refer to a forged will. The use of X-rays, macrophotographs, etc., on the other hand, is methodically not different from the use of spectacles or of a magnifying glass. These devices enable the art-historian to see more than he could see without them, but *what* he sees has to be interpreted "stylistically," like that which he perceives with the naked eye.

The real answer lies in the fact that intuitive aesthetic re-creation and archaeological research are *interconnected* so as to form, again, what we have called an "organic situation." It is not true that the art-historian *first* constitutes his object by means of re-creative synthesis and *then* begins his archaeological investigation—as though first buying a ticket and then boarding a train. In reality the two processes do not succeed each other, they interpenetrate; not only does the re-creative synthesis serve as a basis for the archaeological investigation, the archaeological investigation in turn serves as a basis for the re-creative process; both mutually qualify and rectify one another.

Anyone confronted with a work of art, whether aesthetically re-creating or rationally investigating it, is affected by its three constituents: materialized form, idea (that is, in the plastic arts, subject matter) and content. The pseudo-impressionistic theory according to which "form and color tell us of form and color, that is all," is simply not true. It is the unity of those three elements which is realized in the aesthetic experience, and all of them enter into what is called aesthetic enjoyment of art.

The re-creative experience of a work of art depends, therefore, not only on the natural *sensitivity* and the visual *training* of the spectator, but also on his *cultural equipment*. There is no such thing as an entirely "naïve" beholder. The "naïve" beholder of the Middle Ages had a good deal to learn, and something to forget, before he could appreciate classical statuary and architecture, and the "naïve" beholder of the post-Renaissance period had a good deal to forget, and something to learn, before he could appreciate mediaeval, to say nothing of, primitive art. Thus the "naïve" beholder not only enjoys but also, unconsciously, appraises and interprets the work of art; and no one can blame him if he does this without caring whether his appraisal and interpretation are right or wrong, and without realizing that his own cultural equipment, such as it is, actually *contributes* to the object of his experience.

The "naïve" beholder differs from the art-historian in that the latter is conscious of the situation. He *knows* that his cultural equipment, such as it is, would not be in harmony with that of people in another land and of a different period. He tries, therefore, to make adjustments by learning as much as he possibly can of the circumstances under which the objects of his studies were created. Not only will he collect and verify all the available factual information as to medium, condition, age, authorship, destination, etc., but he will also compare the work with others of its class, and will examine such writings as reflect the aesthetic standards of its country and age, in order to achieve a more "objective" appraisal of its quality. He will read old books on theology or mythology in order to identify its subject matter, and he will further try to determine its historical *locus,* and to separate the individual contribution of its maker from that of forerunners and contemporaries. He will study the formal principles which control the rendering of the visible world, or, in architecture, the handling of what may be called the structural features, and thus build up a history of "motifs." He will observe the interplay between the influences of literary sources and the effect of self-dependent representational traditions, in order to establish a history of iconographic formulae or "types." And he will do his best to familiarize himself with the social, religious and philosophical attitudes of other periods and countries, in order to correct his own subjective feeling for content.[12] But when he does all this, his aesthetic perception as such will change accordingly, and will more and more adapt itself to the original "intention" of the works. Thus what the art-historian, as opposed to the "naïve" art lover, does, is not to erect a rational superstructure on an irrational foundation, but to *develop* his re-creative experiences so as to conform with the results of his archaeological research, while continually checking the results of his archaeological research against the evidence of his re-creative experiences.[13]

[12] For the technical terms used in this paragraph, see E. Panofsky, *Studies in Iconology* (The Mary Flexner Lectures, Bryn Mawr College), New York and Oxford, 1938, Introduction.

[13] The same applies, of course, to the history of literature and of other forms of artistic expression. According to Dionysius Thrax (*Ars Grammatica,* ed. P. Uhlig, XXX, 1883, pp. 5 ff.; quoted in Gilbert Murray, *Religio Grammatici, The Religion of a Man of Letters,* Boston and New York, 1918, p. 15), Γραμματική (history of literature, as we would say) is an ἐμπειρία (knowledge based on experience) of that which has been said by the poets and prose-writers. He divides it into six parts all of which can be paralleled in art-history:

1) ἀνάγνωσις ἐντριβὴς κατὰ προσῳδίαν (expert reading aloud according to prosody): this is, in fact, the synthetic aesthetic re-creation of a work of literature and is comparable to the visual "realization" of a work of art.

2) ἐξήγησις κατὰ τοὺς ἐνυπάρχοντας ποιητικοὺς τρόπους (explanation of such figures of speech as may occur): this would be comparable to the history of iconographic formulae or "types."

3) γλωσσῶν τε καὶ ἱστοριῶν πρόχειρος ἀπόδοσις (offhand rendering of obsolete words and themes): identification of iconographic subject matter.

4) ἐτυμολογίας εὕρησις (discovery of etymologies): derivation of "motifs."

5) ἀναλογίας ἐκλογισμός (explanation of grammatical forms): analysis of compositional structure.

6) κρίσις ποιημάτων, ὃ δὴ κάλλιστόν ἐστι πάντων τῶν ἐν τῇ τέχνῃ (liter-

Leonardo da Vinci has said: "Two weaknesses leaning against one another add up to one strength."[14] The halves of an arch cannot even stand upright; the whole arch supports a weight. Similarly, archaeological research is blind and empty without aesthetic re-creation, and aesthetic re-creation is irrational and often misguided without archaeological research. But, "leaning against one another," these two can support the "system that makes sense," that is, an historical synopsis.

As I have said before, no one can be blamed for enjoying works of art "naïvely"—for appraising and interpreting them according to his lights and not caring any further. But the humanist will look with suspicion upon what might be called "appreciationism." He who teaches innocent people to understand art without bothering about classical languages, boresome historical methods and dusty old documents, deprives *naïveté* of its charm without correcting its errors.

ary criticism, which is the most beautiful part of that which is comprised by Γραμματική): critical appraisal of works of art.

The expression "critical appraisal of works of art" raises an interesting question. If the history of art admits a scale of values, just as the history of literature or political history admit degrees of excellence or "greatness," how can we justify the fact that the methods here expounded do not seem to allow for a differentiation between first, second and third rate works of art? Now, a scale of values is partly a matter of personal reactions and partly a matter of tradition. Both these standards, of which the second is the comparatively more objective one, have continually to be revised, and every investigation, however specialized, contributes to this process. But just for this reason the art-historian cannot make an a priori distinction between his approach to a "masterpiece" and his approach to a "mediocre" or "inferior" work of art—just as a student of classical literature cannot investigate the tragedies by Sophocles in any other manner than the tragedies by Seneca. It is true that the methods of art-history, *qua* methods, will prove as effective when applied to Dürer's *Melencolia* as when applied to an anonymous and rather unimportant woodcut. But when a "masterpiece" is compared and connected with as many "less important" works of art as turn out, in the course of the investigation, to be comparable and connectable with it, the originality of its invention, the superiority of its composition and technique, and whatever other features make it "great," will automatically become evident—not in spite but because of the fact that the whole group of materials has been subjected to one and the same method of analysis and interpretation.

[14] *Il codice atlantico di Leonardo da Vinci nella Biblioteca Ambrosiana di Milano,* ed. G. Piumati, Milan, 1894-1903, fol. 244 v.

The History of Art

"Appreciationism" is not to be confused with "connoisseurship" and "art-theory." The connoisseur is the collector, museum curator or expert who deliberately limits his contribution to scholarship to identifying works of art with respect to date, provenance and authorship, and to evaluating them with respect to quality and condition. The difference between him and the art-historian is not so much a matter of principle as a matter of emphasis and explicitness, comparable to the difference between a diagnostician and a researcher in medicine. The connoisseur tends to emphasize the re-creative aspect of the complex process which I have tried to describe, and considers the building up of an historical conception as secondary; the art-historian in the narrower, or academic, sense is inclined to reverse these accents. But the simple diagnosis "cancer," *if correct,* implies everything which the researcher could tell us about cancer, and therefore claims to be verifiable by subsequent scientific analysis; similarly the simple diagnosis "Rembrandt around 1650," *if correct,* implies everything which the historian of art could tell us about the formal values of the picture, about the interpretation of the subject, about the way it reflects the cultural attitude of seventeenth century Holland, and about the way it expresses Rembrandt's personality; and this diagnosis, too, claims to live up to the criticism of the art-historian in the narrower sense. The connoisseur might thus be defined as a laconic art-historian, and the art-historian as a loquacious connoisseur. In point of fact the best representatives of both types have enormously contributed to what they themselves do not consider their proper business.[15]

Art-theory, on the other hand—as opposed to the philosophy of art or aesthetics—is to art-history as poetics and rhetoric are to the history of literature.

[15] See M. I. Friedländer, *Der Kenner,* Berlin, 1919, and E. Wind, *Aesthetischer und Kunstwissenschaftlicher Gegenstand, loc. cit.* Friedländer justly states that a good art-historian is, or at least develops into, a *Kenner wider Willen.* Conversely, a good connoisseur might be called an art-historian *malgré lui.*

Because of the fact that the objects of art-history come into being by a process of re-creative aesthetic synthesis, the art-historian finds himself in a peculiar difficulty when trying to characterize what might be called the stylistic structure of the works with which he is concerned. Since he has to describe these works, not as physical bodies or as substitutes for physical bodies, but as objects of an inward experience, it would be useless—even if it were possible—to express shapes, colors, and features of construction in terms of geometrical formulae, wave-lengths and statical equations, or to describe the postures of a human figure by way of anatomical analysis. On the other hand, since the inward experience of the art-historian is not a free and subjective one, but has been outlined for him by the purposeful activities of an artist, he must not limit himself to describing his personal impressions of the work of art as a poet might describe his impressions of a landscape or of the song of a nightingale.

The objects of art-history, then, can only be characterized in a terminology which is as re-constructive as the experience of the art-historian is re-creative: it must describe the stylistic peculiarities, neither as measurable or otherwise determinable data, nor as stimuli of subjective reactions, but as that which bears witness to artistic "intentions." Now "intentions" can only be formulated in terms of alternatives: a situation has to be supposed in which the maker of the work had more than one possibility of procedure, that is to say, in which he found himself confronted with a problem of choice between various modes of emphasis. Thus it appears that the terms used by the art-historian interpret the stylistic peculiarities of the works as specific solutions of generic "artistic problems." This is not only the case with our modern terminology, but even with such expressions as *rilievo, sfumato,* etc., found in sixteenth-century writing.

When we call a figure in an Italian Renaissance picture "plastic," while describing a figure in a Chinese painting as "having volume but no mass" (owing to the absence of "modelling"), we interpret these figures as two different solutions of a problem which might be formulated as "volumetric units (bodies) *vs.* illimited expanse (space)." When we distinguish between a use of line as "contour" and, to quote Balzac, a use of line as "le moyen par lequel l'homme se rend compte de l'effet de la lumière sur les objets," we refer to the same problem, while placing special emphasis upon another one: "line *vs.* areas of color." Upon reflection it will turn out that there is a limited number of such primary problems, interrelated with each other, which on the one hand beget an infinity of secondary and tertiary ones, and on the other hand can be ultimately derived from one basic antithesis: differentiation *vs.* continuity.[16]

To formulate and to systematize the "artistic problems"—which are of course not limited to the sphere of purely formal values, but include the "stylistic structure" of subject matter and content as well—and thus to build up a system of *"Kunstwissenschaftliche Grundbegriffe"* is the objective of art-theory and not of art-history. But here we encounter, for the third time, what we have called an "organic situation." The art-historian, as we have seen, cannot describe the objects of his re-creative experience without re-constructing artistic intentions in terms which imply generic theoretical concepts. In doing this, he will, consciously or unconsciously, contribute to the development of art-theory which, without historical exemplification, would remain a meager scheme of abstract universals. The art-theorist, on the other hand, whether he approaches the subject from the standpoint of Kant's *Critique,* of neo-scholastic epistemology, or of *Gestaltpsychologie,*[17]

---

[16] See E. Panofsky, "Ueber das Verhältnis der Kunstgeschichte zur Kunsttheorie," *Zeitschrift für Aesthetik und allgemeine Kunstwissenschaft,* XVIII, 1925, pp. 129 *ff.,* and E. Wind, "Zur Systematik der künstlerischen Probleme," *ibid.,* pp. 438 *ff.*

[17] Cf. H. Sedlmayr, "Zu einer strengen Kunstwissenschaft," *Kunstwissenschaftliche Forschungen,* I, 1931, pp. 7 *ff.*

cannot build up a system of generic concepts without referring to works of art which have come into being under specific historical conditions; but in doing this he will, consciously or unconsciously, contribute to the development of art-history which, without theoretical orientation, would remain a congeries of unformulated particulars.

When we call the connoisseur a laconic art-historian and the art-historian a loquacious connoisseur, the relation between the art-historian and the art-theorist may be compared to that between two neighbors who have the right of shooting over the same district, while one of them owns the gun and the other all the ammunition. Both parties would be well advised if they realized this condition of their partnership. It has rightly been said that theory, if not received at the door of an empirical discipline, comes in through the chimney like a ghost and upsets the furniture. But it is no less true that history, if not received at the door of a theoretical discipline dealing with the same set of phenomena, creeps into the cellar like a horde of mice and undermines the groundwork.

V

It may be taken for granted that art-history deserves to be counted among the humanities. But what is the use of the humanities as such? Admittedly they are not practical, and admittedly they concern themselves with the past. Why, it may be asked, should we engage in impractical investigations, and why should we be interested in the past?

The answer to the first question is: because we are interested in reality. Both the humanities and the natural sciences, as well as mathematics and philosophy, have the impractical outlook of what the ancients called *vita contemplativa* as opposed to *vita activa*. But is the contemplative life less real or, to be more precise, is its contribution to what we call reality, less important than that of the active life?

The History of Art

The man who takes a paper dollar in exchange for twenty-five pounds of apples commits an act of faith, and subjects himself to a theoretical doctrine, as did the mediaeval man who paid for indulgence. The man who is run over by an automobile is run over by mathematics, physics and chemistry. For he who leads the contemplative life cannot help influencing the active, just as he cannot prevent the active life from influencing his thought. Philosophical and psychological theories, historical doctrines and all sorts of speculations and discoveries have changed, and keep changing, the lives of countless millions. Even he who merely transmits knowledge or learning participates, in his modest way, in the process of shaping reality—of which fact the enemies of humanism are perhaps more keenly aware than its friends.[18] It is impossible to conceive of our world in terms of action alone. Only in God is there a "Coincidence of Act and Thought" as the scholastics put it. Our reality can only be understood as an interpenetration of these two.

But even so, why should we be interested in the past? The answer is the same: because we are interested in reality. There is nothing less real than the present. An hour ago, this lecture belonged to the future. In four minutes, it will belong to the past. When I said that the man who is run over by an automobile is run over by mathematics, physics and chemistry, I could just as well have said that he is run over by Euclid, Archimedes and Lavoisier.

[18] In a letter to the *New Statesman and Nation,* XIII, 1937, June 19, a Mr. Pat Sloan defends the dismissal of professors and teachers in Soviet Russia by stating that "a professor who advocates an antiquated pre-scientific philosophy as against a scientific one may be as powerful a reactionary force as a soldier in an army of intervention." And it turns out that by "advocating" he means also the mere transmission of what he calls "pre-scientific" philosophy, for he continues as follows: "How many minds in Britain today are being kept from ever establishing contact with Marxism by the simple process of loading them to capacity with the works of Plato and other philosophers? These works play not a neutral, but an anti-Marxist rôle in such circumstances, and Marxists recognize this fact." Needless to say, the works of "Plato and other philosophers" also play an anti-Fascist rôle "in such circumstances," and Fascists, too, "recognize this fact."

To grasp reality we have to detach ourselves from the present. Philosophy and mathematics do this by building systems in a medium which is by definition not subject to time. Natural science and the humanities do it by creating those spatio-temporal structures which I have called the "cosmos of nature" and the "cosmos of culture." And here we touch upon what is perhaps the most fundamental difference between the humanities and the natural sciences. Natural science observes the time-bound processes of nature and tries to apprehend the timeless laws according to which they unfold. Physical observation is only possible where something "happens," that is, where a change occurs or is made to occur by way of experiment. And it is these changes which are finally symbolized by mathematical formulae. The humanities, on the other hand, are not faced by the task of arresting what otherwise would slip away, but of enlivening what otherwise would remain dead. Instead of dealing with temporal phenomena, and causing time to stop, they penetrate into a region where time has stopped of its own accord, and try to re-activate it. Gazing as they do at those frozen, stationary records of which I have said that they "emerge from the stream of time," the humanities endeavor to capture the processes in the course of which those records were produced and became what they are.[19]

In thus endowing static records with dynamic life, instead of reducing transitory events to static laws, the humanities do not conflict with, but complement, the natural sciences. In

---

[19] For the humanities it is not a romantic ideal but a methodological necessity to "enliven" the past. They can express the fact that the records A, B and C are "connected" with each other only in statements to the effect that the man who produced the record A must have been acquainted with the records B and C, or with records of the type B and C, or with a record X which was in turn the source of B and C, or that he must have been acquainted with B while the maker of B must have been acquainted with C, etc. It is just as inevitable for the humanities to think and to express themselves in terms of "influences," "lines of evolution," etc., as it is for the natural sciences to think and to express themselves in terms of mathematical equations.

fact these two presuppose and *demand* each other. Science—here understood in the true sense of the term, namely, as a serene and self-dependent pursuit of knowledge, not as something subservient to "practical" ends—and the humanities are sisters, brought forth as they are by that movement which has rightly been called the discovery (or, in a larger historical perspective, rediscovery) of both the world and man. And as they were born and reborn together, they will also die and be resurrected together if destiny so wills. If the anthropocratic civilization of the Renaissance is headed, as it seems to be, for a "Middle Ages in reverse"—a satanocracy as opposed to the mediaeval theocracy—not only the humanities but also the natural sciences, as we know them, will disappear, and nothing will be left but what serves the dictates of the sub-human. But even this will not mean the end of humanism. Prometheus could be bound and tortured, but the fire lit by his torch could not be extinguished.

A subtle difference exists in Latin between *scientia* and *eruditio,* and in English between *knowledge* and *learning. Scientia* and *knowledge,* denoting a mental possession rather than a mental process, can be identified with the natural sciences; *eruditio* and *learning,* denoting a process rather than a possession, with the humanities. The ideal aim of science would seem to be something like mastery, that of the humanities something like wisdom.

Marsilio Ficino wrote to the son of Poggio Bracciolini: "History is necessary, not only to make life agreeable, but also to endow it with a moral significance. What is mortal in itself, achieves immortality through history; what is absent becomes present; old things are rejuvenated; and young men soon equal the maturity of old ones. If a man of seventy is considered wise because of his experience, how much wiser he whose life fills a span of a thousand or three thousand years! For indeed, a man may be said to have *lived* as many millennia as are embraced by the span of his knowledge of history."[20]

[20] Marsilio Ficino, Letter to Giacomo Bracciolini (*Marsilii Ficini Opera omnia,* Leyden, 1676, I, p. 658): "res ipsa [scil. historia] est ad vitam non modo oblectandam, verumtamen moribus instituendam summopere necessaria. Si quidem per se mortalia sunt, immortalitatem ab historia consequuntur, quae absentia, per eam praesentia fiunt, vetera iuvenescunt, iuvenes cito maturitatem senis adaequant. Ac si senex septuaginta annorum ob ipsarum rerum experientiam prudens habetur, quanto prudentior, qui annorum mille, et trium milium implet aetatem! Tot vero annorum milia vixisse quisque videtur quot annorum acta didicit ab historia."

THEOLOGY AND THE HUMANITIES
By Robert Lowry Calhoun

THEOLOGY AND THE HUMANITIES

AN ACADEMIC aura hangs about the stated theme of these discussions. To the mind of our day, the humanities appear in a very different light from the sciences. The latter have become so obviously essential a part of our everyday living that we are not tempted to think of them as scholastic and remote from practical affairs. Their more abstruse aspects, of course, are still for experts only, but their concrete applications are visible on every street corner. It is quite impossible to conceive modern life without them. Of the humanities, and not least of theology, this is much less obviously true, if true at all. They build no bridges and raise no crops; they cure no fevers and point no guns. The world's work and the world's wars are carried on mostly by men who care nothing for literature and the arts, and who never heard of Augustine, Aquinas, Luther, or Schleiermacher. The humanities have doubtless a certain charm, as of things old and strange. But this is for people of leisure, with antiquarian tastes. Hard-pressed men and women of the present, at grips with ruffianism in power, faced with possible economic and political collapse, have no time for such luxuries. For those who must carry the burden and heat of our day, the humanities are simply irrelevant.

Like most half-truths, this one is plausible until it runs head-on into a fact. The fact is that, for thousands of years, practitioners of power-politics have tried hard to suppress practitioners of the humanities, and they are still trying. In the prisons, the concentration camps, and the graves of the newest autocracies, and in exile from their borders, are thousands of journalists and men of letters, artists and musicians, historians, philosophers, preachers and theologians. Dictators who pride themselves on their realism have never regarded these folk as innocuous drones. They treat them as active men and women whose professional activities must be whipped into line. Rightly or wrongly, the leaders judge that if dictatorship is to succeed, a people's literature, art, scholarship, and religion cannot safely be left free, lest freedom in these areas spread into others, and make thoroughgoing control of economic and political behavior also impossible. Hence persecution, censorship, and all the modern high-pressure devices for shaping a public mind by mass production. In the eyes of hard-headed dictators, the humanities are not irrelevant.

Moreover, they do not yield easily to dragooning. For all their intangibility, or perhaps because of it, they have in general offered surprisingly stubborn resistance to coercion. Without benefit of arms, early Christianity won its place in a hostile Roman empire, and once established therein, survived the empire's collapse. Greek, Jewish, and Arab learning, in turn, made their way into the stream of jealously defended Christian culture, in spite of the Inquisition and the civil arm. The Renaissance and Reformation had to contend against all the entrenched forces of feudalism, and won out. Gunpowder and Aztec gold helped, in this last instance, but the vernacular Bible, the printing press, and "the free spirit" were no less basic, as various persecuted sects proved. Today, with a new tide of official cruelty rising, the landmarks of human freedom have thus far been guarded most stubbornly not by the troops of the great "democratic" powers but by the pacifist Ossietzky, and the parson Niemoeller, and hundreds more who have only the sword of the spirit to wield.

The humanities can be a sore problem to political realists, even in our tough-minded time. Inquiry into the meaning of these disciplines must then be conducted in full view of this fact.

Theology and the Humanities

I

THE NATURE AND FUNCTION OF THE HUMANITIES

In a fairly obvious sense, the essential human quest is for meaningful and measurably satisfying life. This involves activities so numerous and diverse that they continually threaten to lose themselves in anarchy, which is another name for meaninglessness and frustration. This outcome is prevented not mainly by human wisdom, but by what seems to be the way things are put together in fact.

At the near end, our innumerable activities seem to be grounded in a limited number of basic wants and capacities, a more or less unitary and enduring "human nature." So long as we are human, some things we can and some things we cannot wisely do. Our behavior range is wide, but it has limits laid down in the tissues of our bodies and our spirits. We cannot live without oxygen. We will not, if we are wise, try to live without friends, without something to believe in, without some kind of self-respect. Certain of these limits, like the need for oxygen or water or food, are simple and fixed. Violation of them brings swift and obvious penalties. Some of them, like the need for self-respect, can be stretched and perverted for a longer time, and with innumerable variations. But not with impunity, as our growing knowledge of psychiatry makes plain, and as adepts in the secrets of human life have long known. A man is neither a plant nor a god, and his behavior is in some sense given a characteristic pattern by reason of his being just what he is. To recognize this fact, and to learn more and more accurately what it implies for theory and practice, is a major part of human wisdom.

If we acknowledge then some unity in ourselves, we persistently tend also to seek in our environment some comparable integration, some cosmic "nature" more or less unitary and meaningful. This craving for order appears to be one of our basic wants, quite possibly the most distinctively human of all. Its scope is not at first confined to a select portion of our surroundings—the stellar regions, for example, or the behavior of moving bodies, or the chemical reactions of inorganic compounds. Still less is it, at first, regarded as a mere human habit or convention, and denied objective footing altogether. Such restrictions come only with growing sophistication. The healthy, unspoiled human being seems rather to assume that his environment on the whole—physical, social, and all—is orderly enough for him to understand it and get on with it. Unexpected and inexplicable events come as shocks, not to say as affronts, to his initial confidence. How this naïve assumption of intelligible order has endured both disillusionments and partial vindications, at scores of particular points, is common knowledge. How easily it can be dismissed, verbally, as mere anthropomorphism, is no less well known. No one who is even a little acquainted with modern thinking can maintain such initial confidence uncritically. But no one, I think, in whom it was wholly destroyed could find scientific inquiry promising or practical effort worth while. Our thinking and living, even our questioning and doubting, can seem to make sense only so long as we have a primary confidence that we and the world have each some intrinsic order, and some essential congruence with each other.

In any event, with or without such confidence, we all confront the central human problem of making our lives come out with more meaning than they have when they begin. The problem in practice is largely one of developing a sense of direction or perspective amidst the crowding details of day to day action. Our overt behavior, *doing* this or that, must always be particularized, close-range, piecemeal. We have to do one thing at a time. We cannot do things-in-general, nor act otherwise than here-now, in response each time to a particular stimulus never felt before and never to be repeated. In overt action as such, we are all extreme nominalists. Moreover, since every act once done is irrevocable, in so far as we commit ourselves to action we have to assume thus far the rôle of dogmatists also. Each overt act is like a hammer blow, struck just *there*, with just *thus* much force. However great or small my inward assurance that this particular blow is well placed, or my actual insight into its implications, once struck it has all the finality of a similar blow dealt by an angel or a god. Every act, every decision of mine is in effect a claim to be right.

It goes without saying that particular acts have to be somehow integrated and guided, if paralyzing contradictions are not to ensue. Such integration and guidance is effected largely, for man and all the other living things we know in detail, by automatic controls: by tropisms, reflexes, habits, and other such indispensable mechanisms. Without their silent, swift linking of discrete action-units—a photochemical change here, a cell contraction there, a secretion, a flash of neural impulse yonder—into smooth-running wholes, life like ours could not go on at all. Every decision we make, every voluntary act we perform is undergirded and carried forward on these living chains. Yet though they are more complex integers of action than the simplest units, these chains also are particularized mechanisms, and react only to particular present stimuli. If they were the end of the story, as thorough behaviorists and other proponents of activism would have it, the troublesome question of "universals" would not arise, and human life would be a simpler thing. Truth, justice, and other such abstract words would refer then simply to complex behavior mechanisms, all quite localized and specific; and to certain impalpable delusions of the vague and credulous, the uninformed rank and file, fit only to be played upon by skilled propagandists. The sciences and the humanities alike would then be simply particular instruments in the hands of hard-driving leaders.

Education, statesmanship, and religion would consist in applying well chosen stimuli to evoke pre-conditioned reflex responses.

But to all appearances this is not the whole story. In man, at least, the integration and guidance of action is effected in part by universals or general meanings grasped through symbolic behavior, imaginative and conceptual. By dint of verbal and other symbols, man is able to present to himself as stimulus some aspect of a situation not now otherwise present. The situation thus symbolically taken into account may be past, and now remembered; or future, and now anticipated; or never actualized at any time, but now thought of, wished for, aspired to.[1] Such awareness of universals, or meanings exemplified in more than one situation, brings for man some measure of liberation from the tyranny of detailed stimuli, which act always here-now, at pointblank range. What he does can be done with reference to the past, the future, and the ideally possible, as well as to the actual present. At the same time, it affords some measure of security against the chaos which mere liberation from complete automatic control might easily entail. For some of these meanings run like main themes and leitmotifs through tangled multitudes of particulars: expressions of order in the midst of variety. Recognition of them offers man a basis for living at once partly free and rationally ordered.

The more abstract of these universals, *i.e.,* meanings of the simpler grades, can be isolated in logical analysis, identified, and used in description, with superior exactness. This is so most obviously as regards the countable and measurable aspects of things. These have come to be the distinctive concern of the special sciences, which for the sake of superior

---

[1] How such symbolic apprehension is possible need not trouble us here. That it happens somehow is certain. For an attempt to deny it is itself, if the denial be not meaningless noise, a demonstration that something affirmed not to exist (to wit, symbolic apprehension) can be talked about, critically examined, and so apprehended.

accuracy ignore most aspects of the actual things which men actually crave. Their findings are of increasing importance to modern life, as we have already remarked. And this is not the less true because such findings are mainly of instrumental rather than normative import. The sciences as applied for our guidance tell us more and more adequately how to get what we want. They do not tell us, save indirectly, what we ought to want, or what it is best for us to want. Their attention is focused, moreover, upon some carefully isolated fraction of the world. If they seek inclusive unity at all, it is an "extensive" unity, schematic and abstract rather than concrete.

The more concrete universals,[2] those meanings which approach more nearly the fulness of actual, individual existents, can be attended to and sought after, but not—at least not yet, by us—reduced to analytic formulae. They include the infinitely complex qualitative characters, and notably the values, of things which are lures for purposive activity. These more concrete universals are the distinctive concern of the humanities, which seek to recognize, distinguish, and communicate them in their subtly detailed richness, in such fashion that they can move human feeling and will as well as clarify human thought. In this sense the humanities, as compared with the sciences, are *artes humaniores*. Nothing human is alien to them. They are concerned always to depict vividly or systematically some concrete wholeness, actual or ideal, displayed by man and the world which has him within it. This is not to say that the humanities concern themselves directly with individuals as such. That is the rôle of action, while theirs is interpretation. They concern them-

[2] It is worth remark here that the phrase "concrete universals" is often used to denote *individuals,* of which the supreme instance is the universe itself, the Absolute. Individuals can be called universals only by a complete inversion of the ordinary meanings of these words, in the interest of a metaphysic in which everything ultimately is thought of as a universal. The sense intended in this essay is quite different.

selves directly with what can be communicated, and that is always a meaning, a universal factor common to more than one individual or particular situation. But the meanings which they seek to convey are, above all, just those most complex, elusive ones, hard to distinguish and harder to express, which the sciences deliberately pass by.

It is among these more concrete, less easily formulated meanings that the ends and the norms for human living are likely to find their most important statements. The point can be most simply made by reference to Canon Streeter's familiar illustration.[3] Baedeker's diagram can tell one how to get about in Venice, but it cannot tell him whether it is worth his while to go to Venice at all. Some more concrete interpretation of the place is needed for that: something like Turner's painting, a personal anecdote or two, some pages of Symonds or Burckhardt, or a gallery of Titians. The humanities concern themselves with the colors and smells, the pleasures and pains, the defeats and aspirations that make life worth living; with the interrelations among these, and the recurrent patterns they form; with their intricate bearings upon human capacities and wants, frustrations and satisfactions; and with the world of which they are, in some sense, a disclosure.

II

THEOLOGY AMONG THE HUMANITIES

Among the disciplines thus conceived, theology has a place. We may define its status most readily by noting first its horizontal range, and then its unique perspective.

As to the first, theology has in common with literature and the fine arts, history and philosophy, a wide range of identical subject matter; many procedures for recognizing, defining, and communicating the same; and a special pre-

---

[3] B. H. Streeter, *Reality*, 1926, p. 31. The whole argument of his Chapters II and IV is pertinent here.

occupation with the ends as well as the ways and means of human living. Their common subject matter has already been roughly defined: all of the more concrete and pungent aspects of human life. There is no closed-off laboratory for workers in these disciplines. They are field naturalists, not bench workers. Material for their purpose is literally everywhere that human life is. The time has gone by when it was supposed that only exceptional people and events are worth studying and recording. Indeed, so completely have the great-man theory of history and the heroic convention in literature lost prestige that the burden of proof now rests upon a historian or a novelist who intimates that there are exceptional people. Man in the mass has come to be more interesting, and the common lot more enlightening, than romantic heroes and heroines. We still look for high-lighted figures and happenings, no doubt; but usually with the conviction that they are focal because they are more than usually typical—more plainly expressive of tendencies present, albeit obscurely, in their neighbors also. This may or may not mean a leveling down of the central figures. "Sawdust Caesars" cannot stand close scrutiny. But a Cromwell needs no retouching, and Herndon's Lincoln overtops any schoolbook demigod. What the new realism means primarily is the recognition that the whole lump of humanity is leavened with the same good and evil that makes the front-rank heroes and villains exciting. There are stories, pictures, natural and divine laws everywhere.

To recognize and communicate these universal meanings intelligibly requires the skill of craftsmanship. To convey them with vital impact requires artistry, rising through all the levels to supreme genius. This is true of theology in essentially the same sense in which it is true of poetry, music, or philosophy. A theologian worth his salt requires the same keenness of perception, the same accuracy in identifying and distinguishing data, the same clarity and sound judgment in drawing inferences from them, and the same ability to organize his findings into unified compositions. He requires, if his work is to be of noteworthy stature, a width, generosity, and candor in his exploration of human life comparable to that of a major poet or historian. He must have depth and poignancy of experience as well as some breadth and variety. The simpler tools of logical analysis and criticism, and the habit of using them honestly, must be second nature to him. He must have, moreover, some acquaintance with what other men have written, sung, and painted, as well as with the raw meat and bone of human living; and some skill of his own in translating all this into words, liturgical rhythms, and the less formal but often more eloquent nuances of personal intercourse.

Of the more humane disciplines, history is closest to the sciences in its objective, descriptive temper and its close attention to details, which it seeks to understand rather than to modify in any practical way. Philosophy shares the objectivity of the historical temper, and its theoretic rather than practical attitude. But its range is far wider and its conclusions more generalized. History concerns itself with the pageant of human life in the time order. Philosophy takes account also of physical nature in its microscopic and macrocosmic aspects; scrutinizes the principles of logical method, of experience and knowledge, of existence and value; and continually tries to bring its conceptual lenses to focus upon ultimate reality, the Absolute, or God. It knows nothing in so detailed a way as the competent historian knows his chosen period. It tries to see everything in terms of its essential nature, with eternity or cosmic time ("real duration"), not earthly clock-and-calendar time, as its frame.

Literature and the fine arts, like history, focus their attention upon concrete details; even more minutely, indeed, and with more ingenious camera angles, than sober history itself may countenance. Like philosophy, however, they range through physical nature and the regions of abstract form, as well as up and down the panorama of human life. They seek to elicit from details, shrewdly chosen and artfully illuminated, something of universal human significance. Their media of expression are far more varied than those available for history and philosophy, even when graphic devices, the cinema and sound track, and the dramatic pageant are included among the vehicles of modern historical writing. And more than either history or philosophy, literature and the fine arts enlist the full personal being of the composer, and seek to move the feelings no less than the thoughts of the observer. They have rightfully a degree of subjectivity and persuasiveness which good history and philosophy must take pains to avoid.

Theology stands, in a manner, between these two pairs of disciplines: closer in its procedures to history and philosophy, closer in its intent to literature and the fine arts, and more than any of them directly seeking to move men's wills. Such is its horizontal range.

Yet if theology has much in common with the other humanities, it works none the less, like each of the others, from a distinctive angle and within a characteristic perspective. From thence it must judge both its subject matter and its neighbor disciplines, as they in turn judge it and one another. The crucial theme in all theology is the question of human beings, articulate or inarticulate: "What must I do to be saved?"—that is, set free from self-contradiction, stagnation, triviality, and other forms of death. The crucial answer of all advanced theology is: "Men can be saved only by the power and mercy of God, and God is good."[4] All the

---

[4] Professor P. M. Malin in conversation acutely suggests that this question and answer might better be stated: "Can I be saved?" "Yes, for God is good." To put the question in the traditional form, "What shall I do to be saved?", unwarrantably anticipates a favorable answer: a clear case of *petitio principii*. The real question is not how but whether salvation is possible. I grant the criticism sound in logic; yet on further thought I believe the traditional statement is

humanities deal on occasion with this theme, but for theology it is definitive. A discipline approaches theology in the degree to which the theme *man saved by God* controls it.

The setting of this question and the referent for this answer, needless to say, is the unending struggle of man with the forces of destruction. Some of them are outside him: the ancient forces of chaos, Tiamat, the savage White Whale of irrational brute fact. No need to enumerate them and the brood of troubles they set in man's way as he strives for a meaningful life. Here belong not merely the proverbial earthquakes and floods, the spectacular disasters which overwhelmed primitive men, and which most easily shock primitive-minded moderns. These are terrifying and destructive, but they are comparatively rare; they may in due course become more readily predictable and escapable; and, what is most important, they call out by their very violence the latent resources in men and women, and quicken them to a fiercer life. More deadly than such rare disasters are the dry-rot that goes with chronic scarcity, with unrelieved drudgery, or forced idleness; the inroads of diseases that break down body and mind and self-respect; the blank spots in human germ-plasm that for many make growth into full selfhood impossible here. These are the more deadly because they are not wholly outside man. Cap'n Ahab can face the Whale, even within arm's reach. It is the vitriol in his own soul that drives him mad. When to outward frustrations are added the weaknesses, perversities, and venoms of one's most intimate personal self, one finds good reason to cry: "Who shall deliver me from the body of this death?" It is the pecu-

truer to life. It appears to me that most men and women do in fact beg Professor Malin's basic question, and assume in spite of unfavorable appearances that there is a way out. Some do not. There are always, I presume, a few genuine pessimists; but they are rare. The rank and file believe in salvation, though by no means all of them look to God for it. Many look rather to science or progress or Marx or Hitler. Theology says they are right on the first count, wrong on the second; and tries to say why.

liar task of theology to meet that question directly and try to answer it.

The difficulty of the task is reflected in a certain paradoxical character of this discipline. Theology displays in a special way the tensions produced in human life by the struggle against hydra-headed death, and by the various conflicting demands of actual and ideal, doing and thinking, mine and not-mine, here and yonder. The other humanities describe and interpret these tensions, along with much else. Theology not merely tries to interpret them. It painfully embodies them all in itself. Hence its constant tendency to tear apart into "natural" or philosophical, and "revealed" or dogmatic theology, or into objective theory and "existential" decision; and its perennial inability after all to maintain itself in one of these modes separately from the rest. None of them has ever been able for long to dispense with its other, nor yet to live in peace with it. Theology has for this reason a kind of intrinsic violence which only the tragic arts approach, among the more humane disciplines; and which even they do not match in its insistent demands for practical commitment, and action of various impossible kinds.

Such inner violence is in fact, I think, symptomatic precisely of the incidence of urgent practical concern. Pure theory lacks this sort of strain. Historians and philosophers disagree and divide into schools, but so long as purely speculative and not practical issues are to the fore, each school is quite able to acknowledge the rest as legitimate, though doubtless inferior, variants of a common discipline. It is when grave practical interests become involved that the schools tend to become sects, and mutual excommunication begins. Witness what Marxism and, more mildly, pragmatism have done to philosophy, and "economic determinism" to history. By underscoring practical issues, they have turned peaceful theorists into embattled defenders of some faith. In theology, practical interests are always involved, since the fate of man is its central theme; and the cry of heresy is never far from the surface. There are relatively quiet intervals, like the years before and after 1700 or 1900, when acute practical issues seem to have been settled, when theoretic interest is uppermost among theological leaders, and toleration is the rule. Then "natural theology" has its day. The appeal is to reason, common sense, natural law, and whatever is universal in mankind, rather than to particular insights limited to a favored group. But such periods have never been lasting. Sooner or later the hard-won equilibrium is disrupted. Theoretic calm is torn across by cries for practical guidance and help in the midst of rising confusion. Assurance is wanted, not hypotheses; and theology, always closer than history and pure philosophy to the crude sources of human action, turns again from general principles to particular commitments. "Revealed theology" presses its claims once more. But it quickly becomes evident that this can no more dispense with reason than natural theology can dispense with particular commitments. Unreasoned assertion is not theology, and cannot long masquerade in its robes.

The conflict between inquiry and decision reflected in this alternating dialectic is not accidental, but ingrained in the nature of theology. To examine this last in somewhat fuller detail is our concluding task.

III

THEOLOGY AND THE HUMAN STRUGGLE

The place of the humanities in human life has been defined, after a fashion, and the place of theology among the humanities. It remains to inquire more precisely what theology is in itself, and how it functions in the stream of human living.

It is necessary first of all to explore a little further the interrelation of faith and reasoning, and the nature of revelation, hinted at in the preceding section. Reasoning and faith, *i.e.,* systematic objective deliberation and positive or negative commitment, normally go together in all sorts of intelligent human behavior. One or the other is often ignored or disparaged, but only in rare circumstances actually dispensed with. Theology needs both, and has usually said so.

By reasoning is meant, perhaps needless to say, the systematic employment of those orderly processes of observation, analysis, definition, and inference which are illustrated, summarized, and discussed in treatises on logic, inductive and deductive. Reasoning deals, strictly speaking, with universals and simple data alone; not with things and events, save hypothetically, in the form: "If this be so, then that is so (certainly, or probably)." Whether "this" is so in fact, reasoning by itself cannot ultimately determine. It is a question to be answered, in the last analysis, by observation and faith together. By faith is meant here affirmation or denial, as distinguished from inquiry and contemplation; an attitude or incipient act often called commitment, or decision. When primary interest, as in certain of the sciences and some kinds of philosophy, is simply in what can be directly observed (data or phenomena as such), or in a purely theoretical construct (hypothesis, concept, or theory) by which these may be summarized for thought, faith may seem not to be needed. My notion is that even in such instances the exclusion of affirmation or denial is often more apparent than real, but the refinements of this point need not concern us here.[5] It is clear enough in any case that man cannot live by data and hypotheses alone. He has to act as well as think, and action nearly always has reference to such supposed realities as things and persons. But when primary interest is in persons or an actual world or God, which if they be

[5] I have examined some of them from another point of view in *The Nature of Religious Experience,* ed. J. S. Bixler, 1937, pp. 166-76.

real at all are more than phenomena and hypothetical constructs, faith is present at every turn.

It may be present in any of a number of modes. A minimal form of it is verbal or theoretical assent; the acceptance of a statement as in some sense true. "Julius Caesar was killed in 44 B.C." I assent. The relation of subject and predicate with which this statement confronts me I acknowledge to be a presumably correct account of what is so. But in this instance there is little or nothing that I need do about it, unless I chance to be engaged in historical study or something of the sort. Such assent may evidently, then, involve a bare minimum of commitment. No practical consequences of any moment need follow. If the words assented to are preliminary to action, or if the statement accepted approaches the dimensions of a personal world-view, the case may be very different. But other sorts of commitment than mere verbal or theoretical assent then come in.

A second and a third sort are those characterized by Santayana as "animal faith" and "moral faith."[6] Both involve existential judgments. The former takes a present datum—color, sound, odor—as a sign that an existing *thing* confronts me. This sort of "animal faith" I share with the dog who confidently follows his nose toward a savory bone, or with the deep-sea polyp in James's account, which says without words: "Hollo! thingumbob again!"[7] "Moral faith" is involved when I judge that an existing *person* confronts me: not a thing merely, even a living thing, but a responsible self, bound as I am to certain norms of behavior and having claims upon me as I upon him. These existential judgments may, of course, be as devoid of practical consequences as the emptiest verbal assent. But the kind of affirmation involved in each has its roots more directly in the practical struggle for survival. Prompt recognition of food or poison,

---

[6] *Scepticism and Animal Faith*, 1923, pp. 107, 221.
[7] W. James, *Principles of Psychology*, 1890, I, p. 463.

friend or enemy, is vital; and the commitment involved in such recognition, the readiness to act in this way or that, is the faith we are talking about. How basic it is to normal living needs no proof.

Faith advances to another stage when it becomes personal trust, in which existential and value judgments are combined. At this level, I not merely acknowledge the presence of another, but in some respect I put myself at his mercy. To regard another as trustworthy is to make oneself vulnerable in a different way from the way in which one can be hurt by a physical thing misjudged. Conversely, personal trust when well founded makes for an enlargement of life impossible to the hermit or the lone wolf. Without friends, said Aristotle wisely, none would care to live, though having all other things besides.[8] In such giving of my confidence, then, are both risk and promise. The risk is unavoidable, and the promise never exactly determinable. Faith ventures beyond what is seen and what can be cogently inferred. If I trust my friend, my wife, my child, such trust is no doubt grounded in part on knowledge. But accurate knowledge about persons can be only of past and present, at best, and of these only in part. Trust looks primarily to the future, which cannot be certainly known by me, even as regards those few persons whom I know most intimately. Moreover, my knowledge of them has itself come to me largely on the basis of past ventures of faith in them, when I lacked even the knowledge I now have. Personal trust need not and should not be a blind leap, but it is a commitment hazardous in principle, whose risks and possible rewards, in terms of injury or enrichment of personal living, are alike incalculable.

One last mode of faith goes beyond any thus far noticed, in the scope and gravity of the commitment involved. When

[8] *Nicomachean Ethics*, IX, 1169b.

I trust a human person, or a group or an enterprise to which I give loyalty, my trust is not without reservations, unless I am a zealot devoid of critical temper. No human being nor institution is such that I can surrender my whole self to it unconditionally, without fatal damage to my integrity as a responsible person. Such unreserved commitment is fitting only if I am convinced that there confronts me a Being so great and so good that in giving myself in trust without reservation, I shall most fully realize my own being. This conviction and this self-giving together are faith in God: at once belief and personal devotion to the limit of my powers. In some sense this unconditional commitment includes all the modes of faith already noticed. But it transcends them all, in that in it the ground for all human confidence in general, implied in the other modes of faith, is made explicit; and thereby a basis is defined, or at least intimated, for critical judgment of all sorts of human faith. Faith in God at once gives warrant for faith in human persons and enterprises, and says "No" to every impulse to absolutize such a human loyalty. Needless to say, faith in God also goes beyond knowledge and cannot be exempted from persistent criticism. And if I am critical in temper, it cannot endure in contradiction of what on other grounds I know or firmly believe.

In any of these modes, faith is prompted by what we commonly call evidence. Literally, evidence (*e-videre*) is a disclosure, usually incomplete, of something which would otherwise be invisible; a manifesting of hidden reality by some visible fact. I believe in the presence before me of the invisible thoughts and feelings of another person on the evidence of visible gestures and audible words. These disclose to me, in part, the hidden factors in which I believe. Another name for such disclosure is revelation: "unveiling" or manifestation through observable data, taken as signs of something not directly observed.

If it is to prompt faith, the datum taken as significant must be regarded as having its primary source not in the observer but in the *other* which the datum is believed to disclose. It must seem to be no mere figment of my fancy; not a mere projected wish-fulfilment, however obviously "projection" may be involved. If it were that alone, the datum would reveal *me* rather than some other that confronts me. Confidence that the datum is objectively grounded may be greater when the supposed revelation goes counter to my habitual wishes and expectations, yet turns out to be in line with hitherto unsuspected meanings in my partly understood environment. Thus, the discovery of Planck's constant went counter to the physicists' traditional—perhaps innate—preference for continuity in the physical world: for gradual transitions, no action-at-a-distance, and so on. To all this the discontinuous quantum does violence. For that reason, Bertrand Russell hailed it as perhaps the first genuine discovery (as distinguished from wish-moulded interpretation) that man has made concerning the actual state of affairs outside himself. In similar fashion, unlooked-for heroism on the part of a person whom I have considered timid, or obstinacy in one whom I have considered easy-going, seems all the more likely to be a genuine revelation of the other person because it violates my preconceived picture of him, and forces me to revise it. But such unexpectedness is, after all, psychologically rather than logically important; not necessary to genuine revelation. Essentially, the fulfilment of a well considered prediction, as by an eclipse or an expected act of heroism, may be quite as legitimately taken as evidence, or revelation, of the nature of the cosmos or the person concerned. Presumable objectivity, not unexpectedness as such, and least of all freakishness, is essential to what may be accepted as evidence of a being over against me. And presumed objectivity may vindicate itself in more ways than one.

Reasoning about things, persons, and events normally sets out from particular data taken as evidential, revelatory, or significant. But they are so taken first of all by faith, which serves then as a starting point for reasoning. Faith is likely to figure also as a factor in stage after stage of an actual process of thinking, which is never so austere as a formal exercise in logic. Faith is likely, further, to emerge at the end of a course of reasoning, as an attitude to which the reasoning and its theoretic findings have contributed. On the other hand, faith may of course do duty as a substitute for reasoning, when one cannot or will not think out a proposed problem. In any of these instances, faith may turn out to have been well or ill founded. In the nature of the case, its affirmations are never self-evident. They always need testing. In particular, one must suppose that beliefs tested so far as possible by reasoning are more likely to be safe guides than beliefs not so tested. Within certain areas—medicine, engineering, and the like—the evidence in favor of this supposition is overwhelming; and unless the world is a curious kind of madhouse, this is true by and large. But for all that, faith cannot be simply dispensed with in favor of reasoning, if thought is ever to get beyond pure forms, or universals, to particular facts. Faith is a kind of catalytic attitude, or readiness to act, which at various levels keeps open a way between universals and particulars, ideas and deeds.

Theology shares fully in the common need for reasoning and faith thus working in fluid combination. The data which it regards as of crucial moment are found where human life itself is at stake, and somehow is saved: where sin, disruptive suffering, failure, martyrdom threatens to overwhelm life in ruin but instead becomes a way to unforeseen good. Here, says theology, something of vital import is revealed concerning the ways of that Reality with which ultimately men are at grips; something of the nature of God, and his ways with men. Namely this: from the shadow of death, God can bring new life.

This gospel, common to all the religions of redemption, can easily be sentimentalized into falsehood. The world is not tame, nor is human salvation here and now universal. It may, indeed, be the exception and not the rule. There is something obscene about wholesale optimism, unless the optimist be an Epictetus or a Spinoza, not cheerful mainly about other men's scars. Most men do better to stay within sight of Plato's drastic judgment that "few are the goods of human life, and many are the evils, and the good alone is to be attributed to God."[9] The authentic Christian gospel, for one, has never been complacent about evil, nor sentimental about God nor about the lot of man. It knows perfectly well that the world is not built to our wishes, and affirms that salvation, at least in this life, is for some and not for all. Tragedy is here, and has to be faced. Yet the fact that some are saved, and the manner of their being saved, provides such evidence of the ways of God that tragedy can be confronted with faith and hope, which in principle though not yet in fact is available for all human beings.

If none were saved from evil, but merely escaped it, there would be in that fact no ground of hope for the rest. Luck, not divine grace, would be the obvious explanation; and the unlucky would have no recourse. But in the kind of triumph over (not avoidance of) continuing evil which theology takes as revelation, something more than luck is plainly present. Something more, also, than human prowess, which is itself often the very locus of evil in its most corrosive forms. It is when men are saved, as it were, in spite of themselves, and without benefit of the more obvious immunities from misfortune, that the event can most plausibly be taken as a

---

[9] *Republic*, 379c.

crucially important clue to the nature of the unseen, by grace of which men live.

In itself alone, considered apart from all the rest of human life and thought, such an event could hardly prompt one to religious faith nor supply a ground for theological argument; any more than an eclipse, apart from all other observation and reading of the heavens, could give evidence that the earth is round or the moon a non-luminous mass. An eclipse or a sudden conversion, except as seen in a vast context of experience slowly accumulating in the funded records and memories of mankind, is no more than a startling, bizarre episode. But given the needed context, of observation, inference, and belief, the eclipse or the conversion becomes meaningful and evidential, and can serve to awaken or strengthen far-reaching beliefs. Given the needed context, the exception, the unexpected case, the few saved alive in the fiery furnace of evils, may come to have for the religious thinker a significance comparable to that of a planet's anomaly for an astronomer, or a warped light-ray for a physicist. The exception becomes evidence in the light of which a whole theory, whether of spatio-temporal happenings or of spiritual events and their grounds, must be appraised and perhaps revised. If innumerable plain facts are fatal to uncritical optimism, here are other plain facts equally fatal to uncritical wholesale pessimism. Whatever be the ultimate destiny of the race, and of the universe, here is evidence that there is power not our own which makes for good. How far its efficacy reaches, and what it means for mankind at large, we cannot know now; but we may believe it is far more than we are able to see.

This is what was meant by saying that theology finds its crucial data where human life is at stake, and is saved. These are not its only data, as a glance into the major theological writings would show. But they are the data by which all the rest are illuminated. The fact that some human persons are saved—set free, made whole, or put in the way of meaningful, profoundly satisfying life—in the midst of continuing evil, provides for religious faith the crucial evidence that God is good. This faith theology tries to generalize in the way of systematic thought. It tries to work out in coherent order the biological, psychological, and social factors which seem to be involved in such regeneration, as astronomy has sought to bring eclipses into line with other gravitational and electromagnetic events, as special cases of general and dependable processes, somehow held together in systematic order. The more successful such generalization, the more significant becomes the special case as a guide for thought and life. At the same time, theology refuses to see special cases flattened out into mere generalities. In a sense, an eclipse is merely a shadow; but to say this is to miss the essential point, which is that this shadow appears at very precisely specifiable times and places, and apparently is not cast by any terrestrial body. In a sense, moral regeneration is merely an instance of socio-individual behavior; but so different from everyday, run-of-the-mine behavior that, like physical healing or regeneration, it brings to light aspects of the nature of man and his world which easy generalities about metabolism or social interaction ignore. Theological theories, like all human theories, are subject to correction. Their basic data also are subject to more and more precise scrutiny. But not to evanescence. Whatever they may really mean, they are not ideas but facts. They can and should be seen in various perspectives. But they cannot be cancelled by disclaimers, and they cannot fairly be ignored.

Such data can be directly known to each person, needless to say, and may be for him a revelation of God, only in terms of his own life problems and patterns. They must come as an impact of reality upon *him*. Revelation is not, as such, transferable. It can be talked about, and its import discussed, as blue color can be; but each person has to see with his own eyes what blue color is, or no discussion can make it known to him. There is, even, no way to be certain beyond question that two people see blue color in the same way. No objective test can settle the point. So long as a given person does not confuse one color with another, as color-blind folk are liable to do, we assume that his experience of each color is in general like our own; and we make no difficulty of talking with him about it, and generalizing on the basis of it. Yet all the while his immediate experience has to be his, and cannot be given to some one else.

On similar grounds it is possible to suppose that experiences of other sorts, for example frustration, can be recognized as fact; uniquely felt by each person, yet no more dubitable as prevalent human experience than blue color. Frustration comes early and often to every one who grows through infancy and beyond. It comes in various forms and degrees, nearly all of them unpleasant. Its characteristic occasion is the stoppage of some vital function or conscious impulse. One cannot get what one wants, or one gets it and it turns out Dead Sea fruit. The more inclusive the tendencies thus blocked, the more serious the frustration is likely to be. Familiar infantile reactions to such blocks are enraged struggling, attempted withdrawal, and quiescence. A more mature alternative is some more or less nicely adapted effort to solve the difficulty by manipulative, vocal, or deliberative activity. With increasing maturity, this last alternative comes more and more to be preferred, and in the literature of our day is widely and rightly extolled.

But none of these procedures, not even the last, can solve all difficulties. There come to many, perhaps to all in time, frustrations so pervasive and fundamental as to threaten with failure the individual's program for life, and so inaccessible in their grounds that he cannot free himself and go on. The problem of evil then becomes his problem, in a cruelly trying form. He may revert under its pressure to the behavior of childhood: futile rage, flight from hard reality, or helpless submission. He may, on the contrary, keep trying manfully to surmount the barrier and forge ahead, even after long-continued failure. Exhaustion will stop him time and again, but he returns again doggedly to the hopeless struggle.

For such a one there may come, midway in the struggle or during an interval of exhaustion and despair, an unsuspected, unwanted way out. There may be no cessation of painful effort, no wish-fulfilment in the fairy godmother tradition. The demands upon him are not annulled, nor his failure to meet them condoned. What may happen is far more complex than any of these things. In part, it may be a transformation of his desires themselves, so that without a simple granting of his conscious wishes, he finds satisfaction, keen joy even, in some unforeseen fulfilment less obvious and more fundamental. In part, it may be a transfiguration of the way the world appears to him, so that the barrier itself against which he has to struggle becomes itself a source of meaning, through which he comes to be what he neither foresaw nor desired in any specific way: a self matured and realized. But most basically it will be a conviction, emerging suddenly or slowly in the heat of his trial, that herein he is in the presence of God, and that God is good beyond anything he can imagine or define. The outcome then is "tragic reconciliation,"[10] not wish-fulfilment in the ordinary sense. Pain, failure, and sin are still with him. But they stand now in a new perspective. Outflanking them all, steadily overruling their trends toward disintegration and death, he is aware of healing, saving, or reconciling power which offers him new life, on condition that his immature wishes themselves be transformed, and a new range of possible meaning and satisfaction acknowledged.

[10] J. Royce, *The Problem of Christianity*, 1913, I, pp. 281-2; cf. 309-10.

Such rebirth or resurrection, once more, no one can undergo for another. Each must experience it in his own person. But his individual regeneration is socially conditioned, and in turn it modifies his social understanding and action. As in a school of science, of music or of literature, one learns to see and hear what untrained observers miss, so in a religious tradition one is taught how to look and listen for what earlier generations in the church have found most significant. Such environment should normally help the individual toward his own reorientation. The experiences of other persons, groups, and cultures then normally become for him sources of revelation on a more-than-individual scale. He will see them, and their ups and downs in history, in quite other terms than those of secular power and prestige theories. These latter will still have their own sort of validity unimpaired. Religious insight does not annul the historical significance of oceans and iron mines, the steam engine and the class struggle. But all these factors take their places also in another perspective, of human aspiration, responsibility, and failure, divine judgment and love. High lights and shadows in this perspective may or may not coincide with those seen from other legitimate points of view. In history thus reinterpreted by many reared within the Christian tradition, the lives of the politically unimportant Hebrew people, of the Galilean commoner Jesus of Nazareth, and of the morally equivocal Christian church have become high lights of central significance. Augustine is not alone when he finds in these *the* revelation which most vividly illuminates the entire human panorama and its timeless context for observers and participants limited as we are. For this sort of religious insight, facts are not cancelled. They become luminous, as to an artist's or a poet's eye. Authentic revelation has to keep its footing in authentic fact. But fact becomes revelatory, as we have seen, only to the eye of faith.

Theology and the Humanities

The response by which revelation of God is grasped by man must be a more profound, inclusive, costly commitment than any verbal assent, or factual judgment, or even such trust as one may have in a fellow human being. It takes up even persistent pain and doubt into itself as continuing factors in the basic affirmation that life is unspeakably worth living, because God is good. Such affirmation if made at all has to be made with the whole of oneself, not because one chooses or wishes it with the top of one's mind, but because he cannot help it, having seen what he has seen. He cannot help it any more than the artist can help believing in beauty or the philosopher in truth. In these matters, one lives one's faith or unfaith, in ways that words barely touch. Theology has its roots here.

But faith as such is not theology. That is rather the logic of a faith seeking to issue in the full light of knowledge: of *fides quaerens intellectum*, as the familiar tradition has it. This logic of faith has three basic moods: dogmatic, dialectic, and apologetic, in the old-fashioned senses of those words.

Theology in its mood of systematic proclamation is dogmatic. "That which we have seen and heard declare we unto you." Its starting-point is the stark assertion: "This I have seen, and this I know." But such assertion is not as such theology. An expression of individual dogmatism it may be, but not dogma in the proper sense. For dogma is reasoned teaching, which grows in the give and take of a community, in which experiences are compared and a common body of affirmative teachings (*dogmata*) proclaimed, to which the members of the community are jointly committed. In this sense Karl Barth is right in affirming that all dogma, all approved doctrine, is church dogma; social and specific, never merely individual nor yet universal, in its provenance. It begins with what individuals have seen and heard; it seeks to become universal in its scope; but as dogma it gives expression to the life of a specific community, and widens its range as that community grows. Dogmatic theology is not philosophy, claiming to derive from universal principles and to merit the assent of every rational being. It is more like a body of artistic conventions—say in music, or in painting—which make sense only if a specific community of experience can be presupposed.

But since dogmas are taken as partial expressions of the self-disclosure of God, who is the very principle of truth, it follows that they cannot be merely arbitrary conventions, still less haphazard ones. They must themselves exemplify truth, and be congruent with right reason, though not simply derivative from its principles and procedures, any more than affirmations about colors and sounds, or personal wants, or any other matters of fact. Dogmas must be coherent, and their implications be logically derived, and compatible with one another. In short, they must display system. Where contradictions show up, real or apparent, they must be analyzed and resolved, or at least clearly defined for later resolution. Such explication and criticism with reference to internal coherence involves, for theology, a continuous dialectic. Like all concrete, richly detailed human experiences, and most of all those which try to hold finite and infinite together in one whole, theology is full of antinomies. Its intrinsic tension and violence we have already noticed. What is often not noticed is that the nature of theology requires it to labor without cessation toward the clarification of these paradoxes, without losing its hold on any essential terms. Overt violence is a mere slashing of Gordian knots, a manifesting of youthful impatience or of irresponsible will to power, which solves no basic problems. The violence of tragedy, or of theology, like that of overwhelming love, is a very different thing: a tension sustained against every impatient impulse, for the sake of continually widening and deepening insight. Theology of this sort is dialectical in the most fruitful sense of the word.

Finally, besides internal coherence, theology requires orientation into the general universe of discourse, and the world of all kinds of fact. Supposed revelation must have some reasonable bearing on the facts and truths of the sciences and arts, and of everyday life. To puzzle out such bearings is the task of apologetic, or natural theology, which should meet halfway the philosophy of religion approaching from the wider area of general philosophical inquiry. What is here called natural theology is not a substitute for revealed theology, nor does it offer alternatives to revelation and faith. The "natural religion" of Hume's predecessors tried to dispense with these, and failed. We are speaking here rather of a persistent effort to criticize and test a given way of believing in God, to correct it, and to apply it in the midst of empirical situations of all sorts. In so far as this effort involves criticism of non-theological beliefs, and a reasoned defense of theology against misunderstanding or ill-grounded attack, it will have the traditional character of apologetic. But it may fairly be held that the best defense of theology in our day is a continuous demonstration of the relevance of what it takes to be revealed truth to perpetual human need.

This sort of relevance just now will show itself most effectually in two ways. In the first place, men and women aware of the reality of God are given to a continual insistence that the ultimate reference of human action must be to something which transcends each actual situation, each human culture, even history itself. Things big and little, for such folk, are reminders of an everlasting order against which the relative importance of things present may undergo curious transpositions. In the second place, men and women who believe in God are prone to believe also that God rather than man must be obeyed, when loyalties clash. The driving power that religious faith has given to plain folk more than once has not escaped the eye of trained historians. Some such driving power seems again to be making itself felt, in such fashion that even totalitarianism has not thus far been able either to crush it or to harness it securely. In this dynamic propensity to defy human orders and to follow what for any reason is believed to be the will of God, the strength and the peril of a live religion appears. This is what makes theology practically significant and dangerous, and the need for humane theology unremitting.

LITERATURE AND THE HUMANITIES
By Gilbert Chinard

LITERATURE AND THE HUMANITIES

GRANTING that the humanities are so interwoven with the fabric of society that the world cannot be entirely "dehumanized," a modern humanist can hardly help feeling that his position is far from being secure. In fact, the humanities are attacked on every side; they are losing ground every day; the host of their enemies is legion and their defenders a mere handful. When they are not in danger of being starved and annihilated, they risk being absorbed or annexed by peaceful penetration through the inroads made into their rightful domain by specialists on "human relations," psychologists, educators and humanitarians. In fact it seems sometimes as if they had less to fear from their declared enemies than from their pretended friends. One of the inherent weaknesses of our position results from the fact that humanism is not a subject which can be taught, but a state of mind and a discipline which permeates all human activities. If such is the case, it is of paramount importance to ascertain how this state of mind can be achieved and fostered, what methods can be best applied to encourage it. This is at the same time an academic problem and a very vital question for the future of the society in which our children will live.

I

For a long time, literature constituted the center and the very substance of the humanities. Originally the *humaniores literae* were *artes quibus aetas puerilis ad humanitatem fingitur,* the methods through which children were made into human beings. They included all the studies which contribute to the intellectual and moral development of man, no substantial distinction being made between the sciences, such as they were, philosophy, history and what we would call literature proper. How this empire has gradually shrunk, until the *humaniores literae* have been restricted to belles-lettres, is a well known story into which we cannot enter here. Let it suffice to say that the large domain of the humanities has melted away until the humanists, marooned on an ice floe tossed on the agitated ocean of the modern world, wonder when their last foothold will fail them and disappear.

This situation for which the humanists themselves are partly responsible comes largely from the fact that the humanities have long been considered as the privilege and birthright of a privileged class, and that they have been made to appear the exclusive domain of the chosen few.

During the Middle Ages, learning was necessarily restricted to a very small group of clerics, church people or lawyers, and to an even more restricted number of physicians. Through the discovery of the printing press, learning became available to a larger number and at once exhibited a marked tendency to free itself from theological connections. The Renaissance heralded the first serious break between the spirit of theology and of other learning.

Another step was taken during the eighteenth century when, in the so-called age of reason, learning shook off the shackles of governmental restrictions and of conventional or traditional bonds. The French Revolution, taken as a European phenomenon, consecrated the emancipation of learning.

During the nineteenth century and the first decades of the twentieth, through the gradual extension of popular education, we witnessed a new development: the democratization of learning.

While in former centuries, among the youth of any nation, only a small number pursued their studies after twelve, or at best after fourteen years of age, the present tendency is to increase compulsory schooling to sixteen, seventeen or eighteen, or to make every possible effort to enable the greater number to pursue their studies to such an age. Hence a new problem and a crisis even more momentous than the intellectual revolution which marked the birth of a new era at the beginning of the Renaissance.

The easiest way to solve the problem is to ignore it, namely, to follow the line of least resistance and to continue along the old traditional lines. It is easy to declare that some studies, called disinterested studies, a polite euphemism for useless studies, will remain accessible to a chosen few, while useful studies, studies preparing for life, meaning by that equivocal term, for a profession, trade or business, shall become the lot of the masses. Curiously enough this conception of education which is the denial of true democracy has been presented as a social progress. The most ingenious tests have been devised to determine the aptitudes of children so as to orient them as early as possible towards a given profession, to map out their lives for them and in so doing necessarily to limit their free choice and to restrict the field of later possibilities. Perhaps it would have been possible to make a courageous and strenuous effort to bring the new masses of students up to the old level and to provide them all with equal opportunities. It was much more convenient, for the sake of efficiency and of economy, to declare that culture is "what remains when a man has forgotten what he has learned in college," thus ranking learning as a luxury, and then to favor vocational studies, to make the students think with their hands, as the French have it, "penser avec les mains," instead of thinking with their heads.

The humanists, on their part, were not entirely displeased at the idea that they were superior to the uneducated man, that no utilitarian purpose or aim contaminated the purity of an unsullied intellectual life. Some of them, it must be admitted, were not above the fault of intellectual pride, refined selfishness and dilettantism.

Meanwhile, in the world outside the ivory towers, some people continued to proclaim that it is the right of every individual in a democracy to aim high, that every effort should be bent to prevent the creation or the perpetuation of an economic proletariat. By a strange contradiction, the educational measures they advocated could do nothing but create an intellectual proletariat by lessening and restricting arbitrarily the educational rights of the larger number. If a few still preserve a hazy faith in the traditional ideals and pay lip-service to them, they are most indefinite about the means to be employed in order to return to a broader intellectual discipline.

In a speech delivered at Atlantic City before the American Association of School Administrators, a superintendent of schools recently declared:

"Given a society of individuals who can read understandingly, who can speak effectively, who can write clearly, who can compute accurately, who can interpret facts correctly, who can appraise cause and effect rightly, the social order will go far towards curing itself."[1]

None could ask for a clearer and more comprehensive definition of popular education and of education in general. Only one thing is lacking in this program—the ways and means to reach such an objective; and we should not be deceived by this apparent simplicity. At the end of his life Goethe once said to Eckermann: "These good people do not know how much time and effort it takes to learn how to read. I have been working at it for eighty years and I cannot say that I have succeeded yet."

Such a marvellous humility cannot be expected of ordinary minds and we cannot expect to keep our students in schools and colleges for such a length of time. Perhaps we can at least teach them the rudiments and attempt with them to learn how to read, make them realize the difficulties of the undertaking, convince them that they will have to continue

[1] *New York Sun,* March 3, 1938.

by themselves after they leave college. It is the contention of the humanists that the study of literature is eminently fitted for such a rôle and that it is the prime function of this so-called luxury subject.

II

Considered as a formative study, literature is essentially an analysis of words and thoughts, words written and thoughts expressed by men who were past masters in their own language, whether it be Greek, Latin or any of the modern languages. If properly done, this analysis will soon lead to the conclusion that words mean more than one thing, that even terms used by great writers have to be defined and scrutinized; that even then there remains always a sort of veil between the expression and the reality it tries to express. Language has not been given to man solely as a means to conceal his thoughts, but it must be granted that it constitutes a very imperfect medium for communicating thoughts, and that it can never have the exactness of a mathematical formula. Such a realization can only come through a careful analysis of the elusive meaning of words. Such training is an absolute necessity in a democracy. It is one of the surest cures to counteract the ill effects of mob psychology and to preserve us from blind enthusiasm for mottos and slogans. A humanist may become a spellbinder, but very seldom will he be bound by the magic of sounding brass and he will less easily follow the band than an uneducated person.

What the students of language have known for a long time has been hailed in recent books as a startling discovery. Perhaps it is good that people should be made aware in a somewhat sensational manner of this "tyranny of words"; but is not the remedy obvious? It is not sufficient to ask for better short dictionaries, nor even for historical unabridged dictionaries. The dictionary at best is to the living language what an anatomical atlas is to a living organism. Some knowledge of the value of words, of the part they play in a sentence, is an essential condition for penetrating into the kingdom of the intellect. Words, as Meillet has repeatedly shown, are essentially "facts of civilization," but they should be studied in texts and preferably in texts written by masters of unquestioned proficiency.

For this reason no worthwhile result can be attained by rapid reading. Skimming through a book is profitless; it is even dangerous as an educational means for it can only give this ill-founded assurance that is the "privilege of fools and ignorant people." We should learn on the contrary that the true meaning of a word can only be ascertained from its context, exactly as in a landscape a given color is modified by the reflections or vibrations of the surrounding objects and the condition of the atmosphere. Through word-order the degrees of emphasis, passion, and moods of the writers are expressed and through it the *disjecta membra poetae* are put together. The sentence lives and takes on a personality or individuality reflecting the personality and individuality of the writer. Thus such a study, which is the study of style, enables one to gain an insight into the mind of another human being, much more accurately than graphology would reveal the character of a man.

From this analysis an intellectual pleasure of the highest order can be derived. There are times when the sentence fits the thought as a veil fits the form of some Greek statues, when a beam of light illuminates and reveals the meaning. There are sentences pregnant with thought which awake trains of ideas and prolong resonances in our minds. New aspects, new shades of meaning can be discovered at each new reading exactly as the musical score of a master can never be played twice in the same manner.

Literature, however, is not simply concerned with thoughts; it also deals with sentiments, moods, passions and, particularly since the middle of the eighteenth century, it has attempted to describe the outside world or rather to register the impact of the outside world upon our senses. In the last century and a half, while science was advancing man's knowledge and mastery of the physical universe, no less marvellous discoveries were effected through literature. Our ancestors may have dimly felt awe, wonder, admiration or aesthetic pleasure in the contemplation of natural phenomena; but they remained inarticulate and were unable to analyze fully their emotions. Through literature and through the poets, more than through the painters, we have learned to distinguish and to perceive the infinite variety of the play of light, shadow and color; we have been made aware of the sounds, murmurs, roars of the winds, of the forests and of the falling waters; we have discovered hidden beauties in the storms which filled the generations of old with superstitious fears. Like any other medium of expression, literature has its limitations: in certain respects it is inferior to painting. "When I want some blue color I use a tube of blue paint and not words," Claude Monet used to grumble. Nevertheless, through literary descriptions we have been made more conscious of the beauties of the physical world and our ears have been trained to listen to the voices of nature.

Through literature also we enrich our emotional life. Potentially, every human being is capable of experiencing an enormous variety of emotions. The chances are that this hidden treasure will remain undeveloped, that its existence will be hardly suspected unless some means be found to penetrate to the well-spring concealed under the hard rock. In literature we find expressed, as well as it can be done with imperfect words, emotions, feelings, passions which the average and uneducated man can only dumbly feel. Perhaps in doing so literature increases our capacity for suffering as well as our capacity for enjoyment. It is for us to decide whether we wish to live in rich pastures like contented cattle or whether we accept the risk of a more dangerous but richer emotional life. Most of us will never live as fully and as intensely and passionately as the heroes of the Greek dramas or of Shakespeare's plays. It is only in imagination that we can partake of their destinies. Are we not justified, however, in saying that our inner life will be more abundant, more colorful, if we can perceive in literary creations paroxysms of passions and feelings dormant or inarticulate in the average human being?

In our analysis of literature as a humanistic experience we have so far taken literature in the generally accepted and narrowest sense. Limited as it would be, this domain would still remain extensive and rich enough to satisfy the humanist, if we had known how to preserve it. Gradually, however, and almost unknowingly, we have sacrificed our heritage and paid homage to the false gods of specialization and technique, until in our study of literature we have almost forgotten the humanistic outlook. We have been so absorbed in our work, so diligently busy perfecting our tools, so often lured astray by the song of the scientific sirens, so eager to attain perfection and completeness in our tasks, that the study of literature has been to some extent dehumanized. That we are guilty on several counts has repeatedly been admitted by prominent members of the profession. We have not faithfully preserved our trust and this is the *trahison des clercs*. We have given up our leadership and it has been assumed by unqualified people. We have been too proud to fight our enemies, trusting in the righteousness of our cause, until the time has come when it is felt by many of us that if the humanities are to survive and to withstand the pressure of the utilitarians and "vocationists," we have to undertake a reformation and a redefinition of our disciplines.

Let us say at the outset that we are not so much urged by self-interest and self-preservation as by an ambition to determine what we can contribute, what part we can play, how we can help in the present crisis of civilization. If we accept the definition of Matthew Arnold, our domain extends beyond the dreams of avarice, for the object of literature simply is "to know ourselves and the world." This definition is much too extensive to satisfy our purpose, and is itself in need of a sharper definition. Nor will it be sufficient to say with the same authority that we study literature "to know the best which has been thought and said in the world." Humanistic studies may form the core of a well planned educational system, but the humanist has no imperialistic designs and no wish to annex territories which do not rightly belong to him. We may claim, however, neglected territories and an unexploited borderland which extends between the field of literature and the adjoining fields of culture. More exactly we may reclaim them not as possessions to be exploited under a monopoly but to be enjoyed under a joint mandate.

III

First of all, I should like to submit that there is no unbridgeable gap between the *humaniores literae* and the mathematical, physical and biological sciences. If such a separation exists, it is of a comparatively recent date and is entirely due to a greater specialization brought about by scientific progress. We may divide the works of Descartes, Pascal, Leibnitz, and Newton into mathematical and philosophical works and house them on separate shelves in our libraries; yet no adequate idea of the men themselves can be attained unless we are fully aware of the variety and complexity of their intellectual productions. However, literature is not science and science can be claimed by the humanities only in so far as, and at the moment when, a scientific view, theory or discovery begins to affect the intellectual and sentimental lives of the non-specialists. Copernicus' and Galileo's discoveries cannot be neglected by the humanist for they introduced a new theory of the universe and with it a new feeling and a new emotion so dramatically expressed by Pascal and after him by many poets. In the eighteenth century, the theory of perception proposed by Locke, Hume and Condillac was back of the unprecedented interest in the observation and notation of the natural phenomena and led to the expansion of the "sentiment de la nature," thus opening a new realm to poetry. Current scientific theories are reflected in the works of Balzac. Zola, Maupassant, H. G. Wells, and Kipling are full of darwinism. William James, Theodore Ribot, Bergson and more recently Freud have already put their mark on literary productions. Thus, in some respects, science is ancillary to literature; but there are also cases when the scientist himself enters the field of literature and can be claimed by us, not only when he yields to his emotions and ceases to be a pure scientist, but also when in his observations or conclusions he uses expressions so exact, so adequate, that his style achieves an artistic quality. Such cases are frequent in the domain of natural history with Réaumur and his observations on insects, the excellent Rev. Gilbert White in his delightful *Natural History of Selborn,* Audubon and William Bartram in this country, Darwin himself, Fabre and, in other fields, Lavoisier in the introduction to his *Traité élémentaire de chimie,* Claude Bernard in his *Introduction à l'étude de la médecine expérimentale,* or Termier in his geological and geographical descriptions of the Alps.

The interpenetration of literature and the so-called political and social sciences is even greater. From the days of Plato to Sir Thomas More, Rousseau, Diderot, Cabet, George Sand, Tolstoi, Gorki, Anatole France and H. G. Wells, the communication has been uninterrupted. Here again, however, a certain distinction must be established and a strong protest raised against the present tendency to emphasize the social content and value of literary productions. Literature has never been and can never be an exact representation of society. As a social document it has obvious limitations. For lack of more precise information we have to resort to literary texts in order to reconstruct the life of peoples long disappeared; but we all know that neither Ronsard nor Shakespeare could provide us with an accurate picture of the external life of the Renaissance. Neither Corneille nor Racine, nor even Molière can be considered as reliable painters of the manners of their time. It might even be said that in a more modern period Dickens, Zola or Maupassant could not be relied upon exclusively if we should try to assess the social customs of the late nineteenth century. A social investigation full of statistics and precise data, such as have been printed frequently during the last few years, will provide the historians of the future with more useful information on American life than the novels of a score of writers who have described the American scene. Yet students of sociology have to stop somewhere, and there literature begins. Literature is necessarily an interpretation; but it penetrates further and deeper than any sociological investigation. In this respect it supplements the work of the social scientist, for it reveals not what people are doing, but their ways of thinking and feeling, their dreams, their moods and their aspirations. It serves to remind the public that in the most scrupulous inquiries there is always an element which cannot be reduced into statistics and yet which has to be taken into consideration. These imponderables which baffle the politicians, contradict their forecasts and make the course of world affairs unpredictable, this human element so disconcerting to the scientists, are precisely the stuff from which life is made and with which literature is concerned.

In a similar way there is a close dovetailing between history and literature. If history is mainly a record of what man has accomplished, in literature we find a picture of what he dreamed of accomplishing, of his hopes, of his delusions, of his changing ideals. In literary works we can see how ideas originate, grow slowly and irregularly, disappear or are ignored for generations until they reappear, obtain a general audience and modify society. Thus literature tends to correct an erroneous and over-simple economic interpretation of the course of human events. It reminds us that man is not simply the product of his milieu and external circumstances, important as these elements may be in shaping human destinies. "It is in literature," wrote Professor Whitehead, "that the concrete outlook of humanity receives its expression. Accordingly it is to literature that we must look, particularly in its more concrete forms, if we hope to discover the inward thoughts of a generation."

No less important is the connection between literature on the one hand and philosophy and religion on the other. The humanist is not directly concerned with any particular dogma and with purely theological discussions. Unlike the philosopher he has not to solve the riddle of the universe and to strive to express the inexpressible in inadequate words. What rightly belongs to the humanist on the contrary is the history of the efforts of man to understand the universe, to compass an ever-expanding world and to reach an ever-receding frontier, his yearning for perfection, ultimate happiness and ultimate justice. Without the history of religion and the history of philosophy, literary history could not exist: Plato, Thomas à Kempis, Saint Augustine, Pascal, Kant, Schopenhauer or Bergson belong to us as much as Dante, Milton, Rousseau, Wordsworth, Shelley, Leopardi, Vigny and all those who might rightly be called the metaphysical poets.

It is quite possible that, in order to take full advantage of our almost infinite possibilities, we shall have to modify somewhat our conventional and traditional approach to the study of literature and to broaden our methods of teaching. Perhaps we should pay less attention to mere questions of form, to the framework of literary works, to the noxious and convenient divisions into genres. Perhaps it will be necessary to tear down some partitions and to let in some fresh air. It is quite conceivable that in order to do our part more fully we shall have to require of our students, and particularly of those who intend to teach, a broader knowledge than they have at present. It is to be hoped that history of ideas as expressed in history of thought and history of literature will more and more permeate our teaching and direct our outlook; in other words, that we shall become more aware of the ramifications of our subject and of its connection with the larger body of human intellectual activities, until it becomes clear to a larger group that literature is something more than a diversion and an escape, more than something to be enjoyed, more than a dilettantism and more than the bread and butter of a few specialists.

IV

However incomplete and sketchy this definition of literature may be, we may now attempt to evaluate more exactly the moral and intellectual profit which can be derived from the humanistic study of literature.

Such a training can teach us the limitations of human speech, a distrust of vague words and high-sounding formulas. This result can probably be obtained through a thorough study of our native tongue. There are some good reasons to believe that it is better attained through the analysis of ancient languages and of foreign tongues.

On the other hand, we may go to literary productions to find in them a confirmation of our beliefs, precedents for our states of mind, expressions for our emotions. By selecting our texts carefully we may develop and encourage admiration for and imitation of certain moral traits. It is a matter of common knowledge that certain republican virtues, a patriotic stoicism, have been inculcated in many generations through familiarity with the classics, since the early days of the Renaissance. That this influence is still felt could be proved by countless testimonies. One only will be mentioned here, particularly because it is of comparatively recent date. It is found in the "cahiers" in which Alfred Rebelliau, a man whose influence has been most stimulating to many young French scholars, consigned his recollections:

> This classical culture which was offered to us we took seriously. We accepted it as a faith, a strong and almost unreasoned faith. In us it lived as a body of ideas, of moral, political, philosophical and civic dogmas, which we accepted from an admirable collection of texts. The *Epitomæ Historiæ Graecæ*, the *Selectæ e profanis Scriptoribus Historiæ*, the *De Viris illustribus Urbis Romæ* had created in us a Greek or Roman mentality. We were made able, I can say it truly for the merit was not ours, we were made able to understand all the great things.[2]

Literature as such, however, follows no master and no school. It teaches us on the contrary to discount startling discoveries and safeguards us against the contagious and blind enthusiasm of hasty reformers. In certain ways, it can be compared with preventive medicine. Some healthy individuals can be exposed to malaria, typhoid fever or infantile paralysis without being affected; others may drink, eat and smoke to excess and reach a ripe old age. Some people are so well balanced and gifted with such marvellous common sense that they hardly need an education to preserve or develop their natural qualities. The average man in the modern world does not enjoy such an immunity. At every moment of his life he is exposed to what is commonly called propaganda, he is solicited by politicians, reformers, honest or insincere, promoters and cranks. More recently two insidious diseases have spread like an epidemic to endanger the sanity and mental equilibrium of the so-called civilized peoples: the radio and the movies—marvellous inventions,

---

[2] A. Albert Petit, *Vie et travaux d'Alfred Rebelliau*. Revue des travaux de l'Académie des Sciences Morales et Politiques. Mai-juin 1937, p. 335.

with extraordinary possibilities for good and unlimited power for evil. Against this virus no preventive has been discovered, because the real preventive is intellectual hygiene. The only remedy is not to counteract propaganda by propaganda, but to develop propaganda-resisting minds.

At this precise juncture, the study of literature conducted from the humanistic point of view, that is to say from the point of view of history of thought, can be of the utmost value. It teaches us primarily, in the words of La Bruyère, that everything has already been said. It enables us to travel in space as well as through time and to verify the conclusion already reached in the days of the Renaissance by Erasmus and Montaigne, not only that there is no end to the follies of man, but that he is a marvellously changing and variable animal, influenced not only by his physical surroundings, but by his religious beliefs, traditions, history, heritage and perhaps by his racial characteristics.

V

If no other profit were to be drawn from our studies, humanism could at least be considered as a useful counter-irritant, but it would still stop short of its goal. The true humanist is not satisfied with this formidable array of curious anecdotes, small facts and picturesque observations. If we dig a little deeper, we shall soon reach a more permanent and more substantial substratum of human nature. Variable as man may be, human nature has changed very little since the earliest days of recorded history. Although "mores" are constantly modified, the essential passions, affections, appetites, and aspirations of man were much the same in the days of Homer as in our days. To the romanticist who yearns to escape from himself, "to be somebody else," to be anybody else except himself, humanism answers: "You are also that other man who passes in the street." Realizing that, in spite of the extraordinary variety of man's experience there is some solidarity between ourselves and the other members of the human race, exactly as there is continuity between our age and past generations, the humanist may not know where he is going, but he knows where he comes from and where he stands. He is not bound by the past, but he is aware of the existence of this past, of the part it plays in the maintenance of civilization, and he is reluctant to plunge boldly into rash experiments. He is distinctly opposed to regimentation and standardization of social life, for his whole training has somewhat liberated him from the blind instincts of the herd or the flock. The discipline to which he has submitted himself tends continuously to check unreasoned impulses, to force analysis, comparison and introspection.

From his studies he has realized the mutability and uncertainty of human experience and this is a most healthy and desirable attitude to take at the present time, particularly in educational matters. In a few decades we have seen mathematicians and scientists abandon the theory of the absolute and permanent value of the "laws" of the physical universe. Biologists have questioned theories which yesterday were presented as articles of faith, such as evolution. Laboratory workers, after experimenting on guinea pigs and lower organisms refuse to claim that their discoveries necessarily apply to human organisms. Yet we see that some "educators" do not hesitate to experiment with human beings with less restraint than if they were dealing with guinea pigs, to modify programs and ways of teaching overnight and according to the pseudo-scientific fashions of the day. Because in humanism they see an obstacle to their *libido experimentandi* the apostles of new systems of education have attacked systematically the humanistic disciplines, the study of the past and the accomplishments of the past, not in this country alone but in Europe as well. Nor is this restricted to professional educators. We have recently seen a man, who in his field is an accomplished scientist, lose all scientific discrimination when he ventured into a field with which he was not familiar and proclaim that:

> The child is capable of accumulating in himself large treasures of useful reflexes. He is easily trained, more easily than the most intelligent shepherd dog. One can train him to run without fatigue, to fall like a cat, to climb, to swim, to acquire a harmonious posture and way of walking, to observe exactly what is going on around him, to wake up quickly and completely, to speak several languages, to obey, to attack, to defend himself, to use skilfully his hands in a great variety of work, etc. Moral habits are created in the same way. Dogs themselves can be taught not to steal. Honesty, frankness, courage, must be developed through means used for the construction of reflexes, that is to say without reasoning, without discussion, without explanation. In a word, the child must be conditioned.

If this extraordinary combination of assumptions, experimental and provisional truths and a priori conclusions really reflects the belief of the author, no wonder he called his book *Man the Unknown*. If this is science, I am ready to take back the affirmation that there is no conflict between science and humanism. If this spirit is going to win in education, if our children are going to be "conditioned" according to a pattern arbitrarily established, we can only hope that an ark will be built to save the few surviving humanists in the onrushing flood of scientific barbarism which will engulf civilization.

There is some hope, however, that sanity will prevail and that human nature will prove once more irreducible. It is perhaps too much to expect that all children shall become perfect humanists overnight or even in a distant future. It is not too much to ask that a concerted and energetic effort be made to resist and to oppose systems, theories and experiments which cut at the very roots of our civilization. Our clear duty is to preserve for future generations their legitimate heritage which is the accumulated wisdom of the past. Humanism is not easily defined, but the humanities constitute a definite field of which literature occupies the center. At the same time literature plays also the part of a connecting link between the different branches of learning because its access is comparatively easy, because the first quality of the literary works which are our concern is their intelligibility. The old classics particularly enjoy this quality. They are eminently valuable not because there is a mysterious virtue in Greek and Latin, but simply because they are less complex than the works of more modern writers; because, whether we like it or not, their authors were the first to define the ideas on which our civilization rests, because in studying them we can study our intellectual origins.

Their value, however, is not self-evident. The first task before the humanists is not to fight their opponents with the weapons they are using, but to approach the problem in a humanistic, that is to say in a truly historical, spirit. It is also to inquire into the meaning and value of the humanistic disciplines, to correct and to amend them when necessary, to take stock of the contribution of the past and then frankly and squarely to ask the question whether our modern society is willing and ready deliberately to throw overboard the ballast of the ship and to ride the wild waves in an empty hull.

INDEX OF PROPER NAMES AND TITLES

INDEX OF PROPER NAMES AND TITLES

Place-names and historical designations, such as "Greek," "Revival of Letters," "Middle Ages," are omitted. Titles of articles and journals are not included, but the names of all authors referred to, both in the text and in the notes, are listed. The Editor wishes to thank Mr. J. F. A. Taylor for preparing this index.

Achilles, shield of, 104 n
Aesthetischer und Kunstwissenschaftlicher Gegenstand (E. Wind), 102 n, 111 n, 113 n
Agricola, Georgius, 46, 71, 72
Ahab, Cap'n, 132
Alberti, 62, 63
Alcuin, 47, 48
Alexander, 63, 70
Alfred, 51, 54
Ambrogio, Fra, *see* Traversari, Ambrogio
American Association of School Administrators, 156
Angevins, 54
Angilbert, 48
Apes, Men, and Morons (E. A. Hooton), 34
Aquinas, 121
Archimedes, 115
Aretino, Carlo, 58
Ariosto, 72
Aristotle, 2, 62, 84, 94, 137
Arnold, Matthew, 4, 10, 161
Ars Grammatica (Dionysius Thrax), 109 n
Arthur, King, 63
Attic Nights of Aulus Gellius, The, 15 n
Audobon, 162
Augustine, Saint, 121, 146, 164

Babbitt, Irving, 25 n
Bacon, Roger, 47, 49, 50
Baedeker, 128
Balzac, 113, 162
Barbaro, Francesco, 62
Barth, Karl, 147
Bartok, 27
Bartram, William, 162
Beard, C. A., 86

Becker, Carl, 86
Bede, 48
Bembo, 66
Bergson, 4-5, 23-4, 38, 162, 164
Bernard, Claude, 162
Blunt, A., 102 n
Boccaccio, 46, 49, 56, 65
Bonaventura, St., 102 n
Borgia, Caesar, 63, 70
Boynton, P. H., 38 n
Bracciolini, Giacomo, 117, 118 n
Bracciolini, Poggio, 46, 58, 117
Bramah, Ernest, 7 n
Bruni, Leonardo, 46, 50, 56, 79, 80
Budaeus, 46
Burckhardt, 128
Burke, Edmund, 46
Burnet, John, 18 n
Bury, J. B., 84

Cabalists, 17
Cabet, 162
Caesar, Julius, 63, 78
Calhoun, Robert Lowry, 135 n
Calvin, 72
Capetians, 54
Castiglione, Conte Baldassar, 19-20, 62, 63, 70, 78
Catullus, 49
Cellini, Benvenuto, 69
Cézanne, 27
Charlemagne, 47, 51, 54
Charles V, 80
Chartres, sculptures of, 106 n
Cheyney, E. P., 86
Chicago, University of, 82
Christ, 93
Chrysolaras, 58
Cicero, 14, 48, 59, 61, 62, 66, 84, 91
Codice, see *Il codice atlantico* . . .
Colet, John, 67

Colonna, family of the, 53
Condillac, 162
Condottieri, 63
Copernicus, 71, 72, 161
Corneille, 163
Cortegiano, Il, see *Courtier, The*
Courtier, The (Conte Baldassar Castiglione), 19-20 and n, 62
Critique (Immanuel Kant), 113
Cromwell, 129

Dante, 37, 56, 164
D'Arezzo, Lionardo, 15 n, 16, 17
Darwin, 72, 162
Davis, C. W. C., 50-1
De ingenuis moribus et liberalibus studiis (Pietro Vergerius), 16
De jure belli et pacis (Hugo Grotius), 80
Della vita civile (Palmieri), 62
De re metallica (Georgius Agricola), 71
De re uxoria (Francesco Barbaro), 62
Descartes, 161
De Viris illustribus Urbis Romae, 166
De Vulgari Eloquentia (Dante), 56
Dickens, 163
Dickinson, Emily, 38
Dictionary of Education and Instruction (Henry Kiddle and A. J. Shem), 1
Diderot, 162
Dionysius Thrax, 109 n-110 n
Divine Comedy (Dante), 55
Dodd, W. E., 86
Dodds, Professor E. R., 31
Dreiser, Theodore, 10
Dürer, 110 n

Eckermann, 156
Edward I, 54
Eginhard, 48
Ekkehard of Aura, 48
Encyclopedia of the Social Sciences, 86
Epicharmus, 3
Epictetus, 141
Epicureans, 3
Epistles (Seneca), 3 n
Epitome Historiae Graecae, 166
Erasmus of Rotterdam, 46, 66, 93 and n, 94 and n (bis), 167
Essays and Addresses (John Burnet), 18 and n

Essays in Criticism (*The Works of Matthew Arnold*), 4 n
Essays of Michel de Montaigne, The, 3 n
Essays on a Liberal Education (F. W. Farrar), 22 n
Essays on Educational Reformers (Robert H. Quick), 17 n
Este, 68-9
Euclid, 115
Everyman His Own Historian (Carl Becker), 86
Experiment und die Metaphysik, Das (E. Wind), 96 n

Fabre, 162
Feltre, da, Vittorino, see Vittorino da Feltre
Ferrara, university of, 66, 68 *et seq.*
Farrar, F. W., 22 n
Ficino, Marsilio, 67, 92, 94 n, 117-18 and n
Filelfo, 46
Foerster, Norman, 25 n
Fracostoro, 68, 71
France, Anatole, 162
Franck, 27
Franklin, 84
Frederick II, 54
Freud, 162
Friedländer, M. I., 111 n

Galen, 65
Galileo, 71, 161
Galli morbus (Fracostoro), 68
Gandersheim, nun of, 48
Gargantua, 16
Geiger, M., 102 n
Gellius, Aulus, 14, 14 n-15 n, 78
General Education (ed. W. S. Gray), 35 n
Gerbert, 47
Gertrude, Queen, 104 n
Gesner, Conrad, 71-2, 73, 74
Gesta, 48
Giovanni, Cardinal, 53, 54
Goethe, 156
Gorki, 162
Gray, W. S., 35 n
Greek dramas, 160
Greene, T. M., 100 n
Grocyn, 46

Index

Grotius, Hugo, 80, 81
Guarino, 46, 61, 68
Guibert de Nogent, 48, 53
Guicciardini, 80

Hamilton, 84
Haskins, C. H., 50
Heckscher, W. S., 94 n
Hegel, 12
Helmbrecht, Meier, 55
Henri Bergson. An Account of His Life and Philosophy (A. Ruhe and N. M. Paul), 5 n, 24 n, 38 n
Henry I, 54
Henry II, 48, 54
Henry IV, 48
Herndon, W. H., 129
Herodotus, 78
Hildebert of Lavardin, 94 n
Hippocrates, 65
History of Science and the New Humanism, The (George Sarton), 32-3 and n
Hitler, 132 n
Homer, 84, 167
Hooton, Professor E. A., 34
Hoover, Herbert, and Lou Henry, 71
Horace, 48
Humanism and Technique in Greek Studies (E. R. Dodds), 31 and n
Humanism in Education (Sir Richard Jebb), 16 n (bis), 17, 19 n
Hume, 149, 162
Huxley, Leonard, 33 n
Huxley, Thomas, 11, 33 n, 37

Ibsen, 27
Idea of a University, The (John Henry Newman), 1 n
Il codice atlantico di Leonardo da Vinci nella Biblioteca Ambrosiana di Milano, 110 n
Immanuel Kant, Sein Leben in Darstellungen von Zeitgenossen (E. A. C. Wasianski), 91 n
Institutes (Quintillian), 61
Introduction à l'étude de la médecine expérimentale (Claude Bernard), 162

James, William, 38, 136 and n, 162
Jebb, Sir Richard, 16 and n, 17, 19 n

Jefferson, 84
Jesuits, 72
Jesus of Nazareth, 146
"Johannes qui et Frost," 98, 99
John of Garland, 47
John of Ravenna, 46
John of Salisbury, 48, 49, 50, 78
Jones, Professor Howard Mumford, 35 and n

Kai Lung's Golden Hours (Ernest Bramah), 7 n
Kant, Immanuel, 91, 113, 164
Kenner, Der (M. I. Friedländer), 111 n
Kiddle, Henry, 1 n
Kipling, 162

La Bruyère, 167
Lambert of Hersfeld, 48
Latini, Brunetto, 55
Lavoisier, 115, 162
Lay Sermons, Addresses, and Reviews (Thomas Huxley), 11 and n, 33 n, 37 n
Lefevre, 46, 67
Leibnitz, 161
Leland, Waldo G., 29 n
Leo X, Pope, 18-19
Leopardi, 164
Libri della famiglia (Alberti), 62
Life and Letters of Thomas Henry Huxley (Leonard Huxley), 33 n
Linacre, 46
Lincoln, 129
Literary Works of Leonardo da Vinci, The (J. P. Richter), 104 n
Livy, 48, 78, 79
Locke, 162
Lorenzo and Giuliano, tombs of (Michelangelo), 103
Lorenzo the Magnificent, 67
Louis IX (St. Louis), 47, 54
Lupus of Ferrières, 94 n
Luther, 72, 93 and n-94 n, 121

Machiavelli, 59-60, 62, 63, 70, 79-80, 81
Mallory, 63
Malatesta, Baptista, 15 n
Malin, Professor P. M., 131 n-132 n
Man the Unknown, 169

Index

Marbod of Rennes, 94 n
Maritain, J., 95 n
Marsigli, Luigi, 66
Marsilii Ficini Opera omnia, 118 n
Marx, 132 n
Marxism, 115 n, 133
Matthew of Paris, 48
Maupassant, 162, 163
Medici, the, 59, 69; Cosimo, 58, 64, 68; Lorenzo, 67; Piero, 58, 61
Meillet, 158
Melancthon, 67, 72
Melencolia (Dürer), 110 n
Michelangelo, 98, 103
Milan candlesticks, 103
Milton, 164
Mirandola, della, Pico, *see* Pico della Mirandola
Molière, 163
Monet, Claude, 159
Montaigne, de, Michel, 2-3 and n, 66, 72, 167
More, Paul Elmer, 25 n
More, Sir Thomas, 67, 162
More Contemporary Americans (P. H. Boynton), 38 n
Munro, D. C., 50
Murray, Gilbert, 109 n

Natural History of Selborn (Rev. Gilbert White), 162
Nature of Religious Experience, The (ed. J. S. Bixler), 135 n
Nature of the Social Sciences (C. A. Beard), 86
Newman, John Henry, 1
Newton, 96, 161
Niccoli, Niccolo, 46, 57-9, 61, 65
Niccolo, *see* Niccoli, Niccolo
Nicomachean Ethics (Aristotle), 137 n
Niemoeller, 122
Normans, 54

Odysseus, 59
Orator (Cicero), 61
Orsini, 53
Ossietzky, 122
Otto, 54
Otto of Freising, 48
Ovid, 94

Padua, university of, 68 *et seq.*
Pagolo, 64, 68
Palmieri, 62
Pandects of the Corpus Juris Civilis (Politian), 67
Panofsky, Erwin, 94 n, 98 n, 109 n, 113 n
Pantagruel, 16
Pantheon, 103
Paracelsus, 71
Parker, C. S., 22 n
Pascal, 161, 162, 164
Paul, N. M., 5 n, 24 n, 38 n
Paul, Saint, 99
Paul Elmer More and American Criticism (Robert Shafer), 25 n
Pavia, university of, 68 *et seq.*
Pazzi, Piero, 58, 59
Peirce, C. S., 105
Peter, Saint, 99
Petit, A. Albert, 166 n
Petrarch, 45, 46, 47, 48, 49, 50, 52-6, 60, 61, 66, 67, 94 n
Pfeiffer, R., 93 n
Philip II, 54
Philip IV, 54
Philosophy and History, Essays presented to Ernst Cassirer, 96 n
Picasso, 27
Piccolomini, Aeneas, 16
Pico della Mirandola, 67, 92
Pisa, university of, 68 *et seq.*
Piumati, G., 110 n
Planck, 139
Plato, 3, 12, 62, 64, 84, 115 n, 141, 162, 164
Platonic Academy, 64
Plutarch, 61, 62, 78
Poems (Matthew Arnold), 10 n
Poggio, *see* Bracciolini, Poggio
Politian, 67
Pope Leo X, *see* Leo X, Pope
Poussin, 101-2 and n
Prince, The (Machiavelli), 62, 80
Principe, Il, see *Prince, The*
Principles of Psychology (William James), 136 n
Problem of Christianity, The (J. Royce), 145 n
Prometheus, 117

Index

Quick, Robert H., 17 n
Quintillian, 49, 61, 62, 77

Rabelais, 16-17, 72
Racine, 163
Reality (B. H. Streeter), 128 n
Réaumur, 162
Rebelliau, Alfred, 166 and n
Religio Grammatici, The Religion of a Man of Letters (Gilbert Murray), 109 n
Rembrandt, 37, 111
Republic (Plato), 141 n
Reuchlin, John, 46, 67
Ribot, Theodore, 162
Richter, J. P., 104 n
Robert of Naples, King, 54
Roger of Sicily, 54
Rolfe, John C., 15 n
Romance of the Rose, 55
Ronsard, 163
Rousseau, 162, 164
Royce, J., 145 n
Ruhe, A., 5 n, 24 n, 38 n
Russell, Bertrand, 139

Sallust, 48, 78
Salutati, Coluccio, 46, 56, 60, 67
Sand, George, 162
Santayana, 136
Sarton, Professor George, 32-3 and n
Savonarola, uncle of, 68
Saxl, F., 94 n
Saxon Emperors (Germany), 51
Scaliger, 81
Scepticism and Animal Faith (Santayana), 136 n
Schleiermacher, 121
Schopenhauer, 164
Scipio, 91
Scotus, John, 49
Sedlmayr, H., 113 n
Selectae e profanis Scriptoribus Historiae, 166
Seneca, 3 n, 48, 62, 110 n
Servatus, Lupus, 48, 53
Seven Arts, The (Theodore Dreiser), 10 n
Shafer, Robert, 25 n
Shakespeare, 33, 37, 160, 163

Shelley, 164
Shem, A. J., 1 n
Signory (Pistoia), 65
Sistine ceiling (Michelangelo), 98
Sloan, Mr. Pat, 115 n
Some Problems of Philosophy (William James), 38 n
Sophocles, 37, 110 n
Spinoza, 141
Stein, Gertrude, 27
Stoics, 2, 19
Strabo, 68
Streeter, B. H., 128 and n
Strozzi, Palla, 57, 58, 59
Studies in Iconology (E. Panofsky), 109 n
Symonds, J. A., 49, 128

Tacitus, 18
Talmudists, 17
Tasso, 72
Tennyson, Alfred Lord, 13
Terence, 48
Termier, 162
Theodulphus, 48
Thomas à Kempis, 164
Thucydides, 78
Tiamat, 132
Tiptoft, John, 67
Titian, 37, 128
Tolstoi, 162
Toward Standards (Norman Foerster), 25 n
Traité élémentaire de chimie (Lavoisier), 162
Traversari, Ambrogio, 57, 66-7
Tresor (Brunetto Latini), 55
Turner, 128

Uhlig, P., 109 n
Urbino, court of, 63; Duke of, 65

Valla, Lorenzo, 46, 47, 81
Vegetius, 63
Velasquez, 37
Vergerius, Pietro, 16, 17-18
Vesalius, 71
Vespasiano, 58, 65
Vettori, 59
Vigny, 164
Vincent of Beauvais, 47

Index

Vinci, da, Leonardo, 63, 70, 71, 96, 104 n, 110 and n
Virgil, 48, 84
Visconti, court of the, 54
Visconti, Gian Galeazzo, 60
Vitruvius, 63
Vittorino da Feltre, 16, 46, 61, 75, 78
Vittorino da Feltre and other Humanist Educators (W. H. Woodward), 15 n, 16 n (bis), 17 n, 18 n (bis)
Vives, 46, 72
Voigt, 66
von Hutten, Ulrich, 93

Wasianski, E. A. C., 91 n
Webster's New International Dictionary, 1
Wells, H. G., 162
Whipple, Guy M., 5 n

White, Rev. Gilbert, 162
Whitehead, Professor A. N., 164
White Whale, 132
William of Tyre, 48, 78
William the Conqueror, 54
Wind, E., 96 n, 102 n, 111 n, 113 n
Woodward, W. H., 15 n, 16 n (bis), 17 n, 18 n (bis)
Worcester, Earl of, 67
Wordsworth, 164
Works of Alfred Lord Tennyson, The, 13 n

Xenophon, 3, 78
Ximenes, 46, 72

Zeitlin, Jacob, 3 n
Zola, 162, 163

DE ANZA COLLEGE LEARNING CENTER

3 1716 00300 9135

CIR LC1011 .G73 1969 2ND
FLOOR-SOUTH MEZZ.
Greene, Theodore Meyer
The meaning of the humanities;